For my parents

Illustration for *Superliminare* from the tenth (1674) edition of *The Temple* (From a copy in the University of Kentucky library)

Utmost Art

Utmost Art

Complexity in the Verse
of George Herbert

by Mary Ellen Rickey

UNIVERSITY OF KENTUCKY PRESS

Acknowledgments

Had I some measure of Herbert's skill, I could with brevity and grace indicate the extent of my gratitude to the scholars and critics who have provided readers of this century with accurate Renaissance poetic texts and have done much to illuminate the poetry. I do not, however, and so must remain content to thank those whose favors stand immediately behind this book: the Kentucky Research Foundation, for the fellowship which enabled me to complete it in an interval away from normal academic responsibilities; my colleague Professor Thomas B. Stroup, for his reading the manuscript and offering valuable suggestions; the staff of the Margaret I. King Library of the University of Kentucky, for their many kindnesses; and the editors of the *Journal of English and Germanic Philology,* for their permission to use as a part of my fourth chapter an essay originally printed in that journal.

Contents

Introduction

GEORGE HERBERT has fared much better in recent decades than have some other poets whose twentieth-century lives began in the shadow of Donne. Rarely is he held now to be important only as an exemplar of the metaphysical manner, or found wanting because he is unlike Donne; and gradually, he is being dissociated from the company of sweetly solemn versifiers. One would be surprised, I believe, to hear from a contemporary scholar the kind of evaluation of Herbert's accomplishment which prevailed in the early decades of our century, when a typical commentator remarked that "He is a signpost to be recorded rather than a writer to be read. His work is not only narrow in artistic range, but is marred by unconscious awkwardness as well as by the deliberate mannerisms which . . . he borrowed from the conventions of the hour."[1] Today one is more likely to find Herbert praised, no less for the excellence of his writing than for the sanctity of his life. We are coming to see his poetry as one of the truly notable achievements of a remarkable century, not merely as a Donnian disciple's registration of his inner life.

The progress of general respect for *The Temple* has been helped along immeasurably by scholarship pointing out its previously unsuspected scope of thematic materials. Herbert sings in his meditations, but at the same time, he

says a great deal; in few other English devotional poets
does the idea count for so much. Yet three hundred years
have blurred many of these ideas, to a greater degree
perhaps than they have the more overtly stated ones of a
number of Herbert's contemporaries, and only lately has
critical investigation begun to make clear some ingredients
of Herbert's verse which must have been immediately
apparent to a cultivated reader of his day. The commentary
of Hutchinson's admirable edition opens up whole groups
of the poems. Rosamund Tuve has shown how his interest
in the relationship of Old Testament type and New Testament mystery informs most of the pieces in his volume, and
consequently how many of the passages commonly dismissed
as private idiom in actuality purvey traditional ideology
now forgotten by many twentieth-century readers. Joseph
Summers, discussing Herbert's conception of order and his
adaptations of musical forms, has illuminated the contribu-
tions which they make to the meanings of his poems as well
as to their structures. Marchette Chute's biography, with
its detailed exploration of the poet's rearing and education,
redirects one's attention to the cultivation and erudition
which were his by virtue of his being a Herbert and a
university orator; and by counteracting the unfortunately
tenacious impression of him as a winsome but provincial
parson, her account presses one to read the poems fully
alert to their keenness. These studies,[2] along with others
of lesser scope—many of which I shall mention—have helped
to reestablish Herbert as a writer of substance as well as
grace. The ghost of his poetic slightness bids fair to be laid.

  Repeated readings of *The Temple* have convinced me
that it has yet more riches to yield. It is not with the
intention of revealing an altogether "new" Herbert that I
have undertaken this volume, nor of questioning the
importance of the distinguished scholarship of the last
generation, but rather with the desire of adding to its
inventory of Herbert's wealth. Several of the elements

which Herbert is generally thought to have avoided are, as
I shall show, regularly enlisted in the construction of his
verses. I do not claim that all of these neglected elements
amount to as much in a total assessment of the poetry as do
its Biblical and liturgical constituents or its maker's virtually unique management of form. But to the widening
circle of Herbert admirers, surely any further disclosure of
his material and method will be welcome, and can lead
only to a more thoroughgoing appreciation of the larger
components of his work.

Herbert has been slow in regaining the understanding
of his audience. This is no wonder, really, for the smoothness of his verse and the peculiar simplicity that it seems at
first to emanate veil its genuine complexity. As we become
increasingly sensible of the extent of this complexity, as we
focus upon the individual tesserae of his mosaics, we must,
I think, experience a growing respect for the formative
power which could harmonize this sizable repertory of motif
into a poetry which, while conceptually abundant, is nonetheless unpretentious and even tidy. Poem for poem, I
suspect that Herbert does not lag far behind Donne in
concentration of idea; but though one is intensely aware of
the intellectual play in the simplest Donne poem (even
though he may not be able to follow the fine-drawn distinctions of the argument), he may quite possibly enjoy one of
Herbert's verses because of its neat stanzaic arrangement or
the freshness of tone, while missing the bulk of its intellectual implications. Just as Donne manages his imagerial
hypotheses so that they are conspicuous, Herbert mutes the
ideas which he obviously has combined with the most
scrupulous care. This practice is surely deliberate; and
both his reasons for this subordination and the means by
which he accomplishes it constitute important aspects of
his art, aspects which I propose to examine and to explain.

Frequently in this volume I have cited passages from
Donne and Vaughan in the hope of clarifying some of

Herbert's obscurities, though I have drawn upon each of them for quite different reasons. Donne seems to me the natural forerunner of Herbert to whom to point: Herbert knew a good quantity of his mother's protégé's religious verse, as his borrowings show; this verse enjoyed such a vogue at the time that no serious devotional poet could ignore it, though of course he was by no means obliged to imitate it; and, perhaps of most import, Herbert's methods depart so sharply from most of Donne's that a convenient way of pointing out the singularity of the younger poet is to compare his work with Donne's treatments of similar subjects and motifs. Vaughan, on the other hand, is of great help in glossing many difficult spots in *The Temple*. His enthusiasm for Herbert manifested itself not only in the innumerable exact echoes of his master, but in expanding and rendering more explicit many of his allusions and suggestions. Some of my readings of Herbert poems, then, I shall support with analogues from *Silex Scintillans*.

I have not always troubled to notice the distinction between Herbert the man and the speaker in the poems. Such a distinction obviously exists in many of the verses, and the intriguing problem of Herbert's varying completeness of identification with his persona merits analysis, along with the cognate question of the audience which he envisioned. Unblushingly I have stated that "Herbert says" or "Herbert complains," and do not feel myself wholly inaccurate, since his voice can be heard almost continuously throughout *The Temple,* even though sometimes disguised and dramatically pitched. To attribute the sentiments of the narrator of *Redemption* or *Christmas* to George Herbert is not, surely, the atrocity of labeling Iago's opinions as Shakespeare's.

The identity of this first person, however, is not my real concern. I propose to examine the nearly paradoxical coexistence of complexity and seeming simplicity in Herbert's English poetry, to point out tropological materials

1

The Classical Materials

MANY CRITICS in the twentieth century have pronounced George Herbert's English poetry conspicuously lacking in classical allusions. He is universally extolled as the master of homely metaphor, as the recorder of immediate, everyday experiences in terms of everyday objects and the language of real speech. For such a master, the consensus goes, recourse to the equipment of the ancients would have been incongruous; the "artificiality" of classicism had no place in such art. Every major commentator touching upon the subject assumes that Herbert carefully excluded Greek and Roman vestiges from *The Temple*. George Herbert Palmer commends him for having done so, nothing but nine mythological references in the volume, some "decidedly questionable"; George Williamson, Austin Warren, and Douglas Bush propose that Herbert avoided classical materials in his sacred verse in imitation of Donne, who, they say, felt distaste for such materials in the poetry of the Elizabethans; Joseph Summers and Marchette Chute feel that Herbert judged them unsuitable for Christian devotions.[1]

This view has not been seriously challenged, though a handful of additions to Palmer's list have appeared since 1905, and though scholars have discovered a great deal in Herbert's verse that nineteenth-century readers failed to notice. I feel that a challenge is overdue. To overlook the classical materials in *The Temple* is, I am convinced, to miss an important part of Herbert's effort to enlist all of his mental resources in the service and praise of God. One element of these resources was his knowledge of the life and art of the ancients; this, he used as tellingly as he did his familiarity with the English Church, the natural world, or the teachings of the Fathers.

That Donne's anti-classicism set a model for his followers is, I might observe, a false premise. Certainly no one could dispute the fact that Donne's mythological references are used in a manner quite different from those of, say, Sidney or Spenser or even Raleigh; but to deny their existence or their abundance is to tread on dangerous ground indeed. A most cursory reading of his verse has brought to my eye a hundred-and-seventy-odd allusions to over a hundred classical figures and places, occurring in seventy-odd poems.[2] I am sure that I have missed some. Even so, however, this admittedly incomplete list should serve to indicate that Donne did not feel "disdain for classical allusions," as Williamson claims, and, consequently, that whatever influence he may have had on Herbert and other seventeenth-century poets did not encourage them to ignore the ancients. Herbert certainly did not.

BUT TO BEGIN at the very beginning of *The Temple*. Since its appearance, readers have been aware of the ambiguity of its title. Modern commentators have had a good bit to say about the word *temple,* some of which has added hitherto overlooked, and, by exploring the development of his art and his own statements about the nature of divine poetry, to show his endeavor to concentrate a great store of motifs in small and unpretentious verses. In the very smoothness of this concentration, he succeeded so well that whole categories of materials have escaped the modern eye. It is with one of these categories, the classical materials, that we shall begin.

substantially to our understanding of both the plan of the whole work and the functions of its individual poems. Edward Dowden, writing during a period when nearly everyone was essentially embarrassed by Herbert's verse but in sympathy with his sweetness of character, regarded the title as too grandiose to have been intended by one of Herbert's simplicity and felt that it was probably devised by Nicholas Ferrar (it does not appear in the Williams MS.).[3] Miss Helen C. White, like most present-day critics, accepts the title as the author's and comes close to reading it as a specification of the Church of England or at least a typical English church. She concludes that the poems were originally intended to give the reader a tour through the church and through the liturgical year, a plan which Herbert abandoned for a looser kind of association of small groups of poems.[4] Joseph Summers, rejecting this idea, sees the temple of the title as a symbol for the body, particularly that of the Christian as he stands in relationship to God and the divine body of Christ. *The Temple,* he feels, is intended as a record of the typical Christian life within the church, a record of the living temple of the Holy Spirit. Quite recently, a completely different interpretation has been attached to the title and so to the structure of the whole work.[5] John David Walker finds the word *temple* suggestive of the Hebraic edifice, going so far as to assert that "The physical structure of the Hebraic temple and the symbolism associated with it actually did exert a dominant influence on the structure of Herbert's *Temple*."[6] His argument rests upon paralleling the three divisions of Herbert's book—"The Church-porch," "The Church," and "The Church Militant"—with the three spatial divisions of the Old Testament structure—the porch or court, the holy place, and the holy of holies.

Obviously one cannot believe all of these theories. In the first place, Herbert probably named his own volume; Hutchinson has described the Bodleian MS. (which does

contain the title and the epigraph from the Psalms—"In his
Temple doth every man speak of his honour") and concludes that it is a fair copy, indeed, a scrupulously fair one,
of the "little book" which Herbert sent to Ferrar by
Edmund Duncon.[7] There is little reason to suspect that the
copyist, probably a member of the Little Gidding community, would undertake to give such an out-of-the-way
title to a work which he was trying to reproduce faithfully.
Surely the ambiguous heading was Herbert's, then, and so
the investigation of its meaning is no hunt for a will-o'-the-
wisp.

The conclusions of Miss White and Summers are not,
I think, mutually exclusive and both, I feel, measurably
help the careful reader of Herbert's verse. For the framework in which Herbert's "typical" Christian operates is
undeniably Anglican, as Miss White says; and the experiences revealed in the poems are so personal that one must
regard them as autobiographical in some measure, though
doing so need not, surely, obligate one to read them in some
sequence and find a "story" of Herbert's spiritual struggles,
as Palmer did. On the other hand, Summers' equation of
the temple and the Christian must certainly have been
intended by the poet, as many of the poems, particularly
those dealing with various parts of the interior of the
church, show; and this critic's explanation of what are
frequently read as the formless parts of *The Temple* as
Herbert's dramatization of the inevitable peaks and valleys
of the religious sensibility is both satisfying and illumi-
nating.

Walker's theory seems unlikely to me. Only two of
Herbert's divisions are spatial; and any attempt to identify
"The Church Militant," that least devotional of the units,
with the holy of holies seems doomed, even though an ark
is mentioned in lines 19-26 of "The Church Militant," as
he points out![8] And yet unconvincing as is his speculation
about the structure of the whole, the title indisputably

suggests the place of worship of the Old Testament, at the same time that it does the living temple of the Pauline epistles. Most probably this was a part of Herbert's intention. For a substantial number of the poems in *The Temple* are "about" the relationship of the two temples: the Covenant of Works of the Old Testament, with its observances centered first in the tabernacle and then in the temple, is superseded by the Covenant of Grace of the New, with its substitution of the human heart as fountainhead of devotion. This theme recurs persistently, furnishing the central statement of many poems: of *The Altar, Redemption, Sepulchre, Easter-wings, Faith, The H. Communion, Sunday, Anagram of the Virgin Marie, Sighs and Grones, The World, Decay, Sion, The Bunch of Grapes, Love Unknown, Justice* (II), *The Holdfast, Praise* (II), *The Jews, Joseph's Coat, Aaron, Discipline*. With this plentitude of variations on the theme, Herbert must certainly have intentionally and designedly have chosen a title for his book that would signal both sides of the Works-Grace comparison. That it did so in the seventeenth century is best evidenced by the modest name which Christopher Harvey chose for his imitation of *The Temple: The Synagogue, or The Shadow of The TEMPLE, Sacred Poems and Private Ejaculations in Imitation of Mr. George Herbert*. Harvey's poems, bound with *The Temple* from 1641 through the rest of the century, must surely have served to remind Herbert's readers of this Hebrew aspect of the title's significance.

Yet another meaning of *temple* was as widely recognized in Herbert's time as it is in our own. Then as now, the word carried the signification of a classical structure for pagan worship. I believe Herbert to have been fully aware of this connotation, and to have intended it to be conveyed to his readers along with the other cargoes of the word. As I shall be at pains to show, classical materials comprise a significant ingredient of *The Temple;* and they are made to operate much the same as do Old Testament precepts, both being shown inferior to the New Testament relationship between God and man. The temple as *fanum* blessed for Christian worship gives as true an indication of the contents as does the idea of the building in Jerusalem or that of human being as living temple. Herbert effected, I believe, the kind of transformation which Ben Jonson attributed to Sir John Beaumont in a poem commending his *Bosworth-field* (1629): "And like a hallow'd Temple, free from taint / Of Ethnicisme, makes his Muse a Saint."[9]

Certain aspects of the structure of *The Temple,* particularly the nature and sequence of its opening poems, can be explained only in light of this meaning. In the Bodleian MS., "The Church-porch" bears the subtitle "Perirrhanterium" (an appellation attached in the Williams MS. to the first stanza of the *Superliminare,* which stands between "The Church-porch" and "The Church"). This Greek term denotes a sprinkling brush used for pre-ceremonial symbolic cleansing. The brush, originally a classical utensil was, it is true, later used in Roman Catholic lustrations. The word *perirrhanterium,* however, is quite explicit; Herbert uses it to name the Greek artifact and to suggest the Greek ceremonial practice. Had he wanted to suggest Roman Catholic custom, he would have used the Latin word *aspergillum.* His instrument of cleansing is the collection of ethical injunctions comprised in "The Church-porch," which, if followed by his fictional visitor, would enable him through his own efforts to achieve chastity, sobriety, frugality of diet, truthfulness, industry, modesty, humility, cleanliness, and generosity to the poor. These are the qualities which, actually practiced by the Christian, prepare him for entering the church proper, and which, by implication, transcend the ancients' passive acceptance of pre-liturgical sprinkling.

Superliminare, which follows "The Church-porch," continues the metaphor of the perirrhanterium. In this

inscription, Herbert combines classical and Christian proscriptions for the use of his temple:

> Thou, whom the former precepts have
> Sprinkled and taught, how to behave
> Thy self in church; approach, and taste
> The churches mysticall repast.

> Avoid, Profanenesse; come not here:
> Nothing but holy, pure, and cleare
> Or that which groneth to be so,
> May at his perill further go. (25)[10]

A. D. commented in 1952 that Herbert must surely have
been aware of the *procul este profani* as the regular beginning of Roman rituals, and so knowingly to have used its
close translation in the first line of the second quatrain.
A. D. further felt that the poet was directly conscious of
the passage in *Aeneid* VI. 258 ff., where the Sybil addresses
Aeneas and his company as they approach to worship:

> "Procul o, procul este, profani,"
> conclamat vates, "totoque absistite luco,
> tuque invade viam, vaginaque eripe ferrum:
> nunc animis opus, Aenea, nunc pectore firmo."[11]

Trans. "Depart, O depart, profane ones," cried the seeress,
"and wholly withdraw from the grove; and you,
Aeneas, undertake the way, and rip your sword from
its sheath; now you will need stoutness of heart, now
you will need courage."

Almost equally close to Herbert's poem is another widely
circulated classical model, one of the verses of the *Greek
Anthology*: "The holy places of the gods are open to the
righteous, nor have they any need of lustration; no defile-
ment touches virtue. But thou who are evil at heart,
depart; for never by sprinkling thy body shalt thou cleanse
thy soul."[12]

A parallel to this tradition was almost certainly in-

tended by Herbert; the placing of this inscription on the
lintel of a *temple* can be no accident. He might well have
known of similar adaptations of the *procul este profani* by
his own countrymen. Perhaps he had seen the work of
William Alabaster, who, at Cambridge in 1597, had attracted much attention by his conversion to Romanism,
but who, by the time that Herbert was at the university,
had returned to the Anglican communion and had taken a
parish in Hertfordshire. His manuscript poems were at
Cambridge—possibly seen by Herbert, seen at any rate by
Herrick, who was at Cambridge when Herbert was and
who praised Alabaster warmly.[13] One of Alabaster's sonnets,
a notably good one, makes use of the *procul este profani*
(and several other classical motifs) in a fervent Christian
poem:

> I sing of Christ, O endless argument,
> Profaner thoughts and ears begone, begone,
> Lest thunder push down your presumption.
> I sing of Christ, let many worlds be lent
> To enrobe my thoughts with all their ornament,
> And tongues of men and angels join in one,
> To spread the carpets of invention
> Before the eyes of all the firmament.
> The temple where I sing is heaven, the choir
> Are my soul's powers, the book's a living story,
> Each takes his tune, but with a low retire,
> That modesty may after reach his glory.
> And let the humble bass beneath begin
> To show how he descended for our sin.[14]

Or doubtless Herbert had read the prefatory material
to that superficially most classical of English sacred works
of his time, Joshua Sylvester's translation of Du Bartas—so
overtly classical that Sylvester thought it necessary to append a glossary of Greek and Latin proper names for his
readers! Among the various preliminary poems to *Divine*

Weekes and Workes, Sylvester includes a warning sonnet which the printer placed under a Roman arch:

INDIGNIS

Hence profane Hands, Factors for Hearts profane:
Hence hissing *Atheists,* Hellish Misse-Creants:
Hence Buzzard Kites, dazled with Beauties glance:
Hence itching Eares, with Toyes and Tales up-tane:

Hence Green-sick Wits, that rellish nought but bane:
Hence dead-live Idiots, drown'd in Ignorance:
Hence wanton *Michols,* that deride my Dance:
Hence *Mimike* Apes, vaine *Follies* Counter-pane:

Hence prying *Critikes,* carping past your Skill:
Hence dull Concepts, that have no true Discerning:
Hence envious *Momes,* converting Good to Ill:
Hence all at-once, that lack (or love not) Learning:

Hence All un-holy, from the *Worlds Birth* Feast
Urania's Grace brooks no unworthy Guest.[15]

And had Herbert lived a normal lifespan, he would surely have been struck by the beginnings of *L'Allegro* and *Il Penseroso,* which follow, of course, a similar convention.

In *Superliminare* Herbert makes an important qualification of the *procul este profani,* whether he intends to deviate from the words of Vergil's Sybil, or from a more general tradition; the temple of God, fortunately, is not for the wholly pure, but also for him "which groneth to be so" —a merciful provision which makes his poem an invitation rather than a warning. Herbert reminds us, in short, of classical worship in classical temples, but his real purpose in so doing is to show the ineffable superiority of the Christian religion, which admits the faulty and which promises succor to those seeking the life of the spirit.

The first poem of "The Church," the central section of *The Temple,* is *The Altar.* In no Christian church, of course, does one find this fixture immediately inside the entrance, and upon reading the *Superliminare* one has figuratively gone through the door. But in a classical temple, the altar *is* the first object that meets the eye. Even Christopher Harvey, whose imitations of Herbert reveal his blindness to many qualities of his verse, realized the inappropriateness of this poem's position in an allegory of the Christian church. In *The Synagogue,* a painstakingly literal tour through an English church, he arranged his verses in an order reflecting the actual placement of the furniture: in sequence, the early poems in his volume are *The Church-yard, The Church-Gate, The Church-Walls, The Church, The Church-Porch, Church-Utensils, The Font, The Reading-Pue, The Book of Common Prayer, The Bible, The Pulpit, The Communion-Table.*[16]

That Herbert's poem should bear the name *Altar* further indicates departure from Anglican tradition of his time, which prescribed *holy table* or *communion table* for that fixture of the church. *Altar* was then a word associated with classical and Hebrew ceremony, both of which have their symbolic places in this poem. But the very appearance of the verse would suggest the former to almost any seventeenth-century reader, for Herbert shaped his poem to resemble a Greek type introduced to the English public in the middle of the preceding century.[17] Two poems shaped like altars appeared in the *Greek Anthology,* which went through five English editions between 1555 and 1600 —one by Besantinus, celebrating a structure purportedly built by the Muses, and one by Dosiadas, in honor of an altar erected by Jason. The altar pattern itself, then, would have been firmly established as classical in the minds of the cultivated. There were, in addition, several imitations by English poets, all probably known to Herbert. The first was the work of Richard Willys, whose *Poematum liber ad Gulielmum Bar. Burghleium Auratum nobilis ordinis equi-dem sereniss. reg. consiliarum ac summum Angliae quaes-*

torem (1573) included eight shaped poems, five mimetic of forms from the *Greek Anthology,* four of them with Greek subtitles. Willys's altar, like his other patterned verse, seems to exist almost solely for the purpose of allowing its maker to adapt a pagan convention to Christian uses:

ARA
CHRISTIANAE RELIGIONI
Sancto renatus infans
Baptismatis lauachro
Deinde CONfirmatus in vera
Fide sacrata Praesulis manu,
Et lectus in sortum Deipuer:
AETATE vernali procellosus
Nostri per undas Ponti
Finesque Brabantinus
Rheni per oras late
Celsas & inter Alpes,
Taurumq' Appenninq'
Iuga Aetuscas urbis
Fassus plolTON Antis
Sactū ac tremedū nōen:
Adultus inter GALLIC Anas
Neces professus CHRISTIANum,
Vir CHRISTIANA Religione.
Ruam scelestus? Derelinquam
Senex? mori ab meme ante malim.[18]

Trans. I, as an infant, reborn in the holy washing of baptism, then confirmed in the true faith by the consecrated hand of the bishop and chosen by lot as a child of God. In the springtime of my life a tempestuous Brabantine, tossed through the waves and along the shores of our sea, far and wide through the Rhineland and among the lofty alps, both Taurus and Appenines, and among Tuscan cities, having confessed the holy and fearful name of God. As a fullgrown man among Gallic slaughter, having professed Christianity, a man in the Christian re-

ligion. Shall I fall accursed? In old age, shall I
abandon it? I would rather die first by my own
hand.

A similar motive seems to have prompted the composition of the twelve altars at the beginning of Sylvester's
translation of Du Bartas, nine of which are dedicated to the
Muses, three of which involve praise of King James, to
whom the work is dedicated. Sylvester's purpose seems fairly
clear: in his translation he means to employ all of the
graceful embellishments of the ancients to beautify his
divine poem. He will, he explains in the altar poems, have
the inspiration of the daughters of Jove—but much more.
The help of the classical nine is but prelude to that of Du
Bartas's much-praised heavenly muse, which Sylvester felt
he had inherited. Here again, then, as in Willys, one finds
the overtly classical used as Christian implement.

William Browne wrote an altar poem and placed it
following the fourth eclogue of his *Shepherd's Pipe* (1614).
A memorial to Thomas Manwood, it is classical in shape
and purportedly composed with the aid of the Muses. It
concludes:

> For whose *Eternity* on earth, my Muse
> To build this *Altar,* did her best skill use:
> And that you, I, and all that held him dear,
> Our tears and sighs might freely offer here.[19]

One other notable altar may have been in the minds
of Herbert's audience, the anonymous one in Francis
Davison's *Poetical Rhapsody* (1602, 1608, 1611, 1621).
Indeed, because of the widespread circulation of the vol-
ume, it might have been the one most familiar even to
readers of devotional verse. Unlike the earlier ones by
English writers, it strikes no Christian overtones: it is a
would-be witty, brittle denunciation of the divinity of love.
Certain features of the poem, however, are so suggestive of
Herbert's later hieroglyph that it seems possible he intended

his Christian altar as recognizable parody of this secular one. Perhaps it might be worthwhile to quote the poem in full:

An Altare and Sacrifice to Disdaine, for freeing
him from loue.

My Muse by thee restor'd to life,
To thee Disdaine, this Altare reares,
Whereon she offers causelesse strife,
Self-spending sighs, and bootlesse teares

Long Sutes in vaine,
Hate for Good will:
Still-dying paine,
Yet living still.
Selfe-louing pride,
Lookes coyly strange,
Will Reasons guide
Desire of change.
And last of all,
Blinde Fancies fire:
False Beauties thrall,
That bindes desire.

All these I offer to Disdaine,
By whome I liue from fancie free.
With vow, that if I loue againe,
My life the sacrifice shall be.

Vicimus & domitum pedibus calcamus amorem.[20]

Until the publication of *The Temple,* then, verse printed in the form of altars had been either wholly classical, as is true of those of the *Greek Anthology* and the one in Davison's collection, or in patently classical forms used in the service of Christian themes, such as those of Willys and Sylvester.

As early as 1610, when Herbert sent the two New Year's sonnets to his mother, he seemed interested in a similar transformation:

Doth Poetry
Wear *Venus* Livery? only serve her turn?
Why are not *Sonnets* made of thee? and layes
Upon thy altar burnt?   (206)

Perhaps the mention of the altar here is merely a trope
which Herbert forgot as soon as he dispatched his letter to
Lady Danvers. But perhaps not. Possibly the idea of the
baptizing of Venus's cult remained with him until he began
work on *The Temple.* In any event, he used a shaped
altar as the first poem in "The Church" section of his
volume. It must long have been his intention to do so,
since the verse occupies this position in both the Williams
and the Bodleian MSS. While clearly superior to the
previous poems of this type, it is, and is intended to appear,
squarely in their tradition:

A broken ALTAR, Lord, thy servant reares,
Made of a heart, and cemented with teares:
Whose parts are as thy hand did frame,
No workmans tool hath touch'd the same.
A HEART alone
Is   such   a   stone,
As   nothing   but
Thy pow'r doth cut.
Wherefore each part
Of my hard heart
Meets in this frame,
To praise thy Name.
That if I chance to hold my peace,
These stones to praise thee may not cease.
O let thy blessed SACRIFICE be mine,
And sanctifie this ALTAR to be thine. (26)

Hutchinson has commented on the form of the piece: "The
poem, as written in the MSS. and printed in *1633,* follows
the shape of a classical altar. From 1634 to 1667 the shape
is further emphasized by lines drawn round the poem (cf.
this frame, l. 11). The lines are replaced from 1674 by an

engraving of a full-length Christian altar under a classical canopy, with the poem set under the canopy."[21] Herbert's first editors, to whom we owe so much for their careful reproduction of his text, apparently recognized the significance of his form and took pains in later printings to make this significance even more clear to his readers.

Conceivably, as I have hinted above, Herbert intended his poem as explicit reworking of the *Poetical Rhapsody* shaped verse. The beginnings of the two bear pointed resemblance; both end with a statement of the nature of the sacrifices; and Herbert seems to parallel the catalogue of offerings made by the *auctor ignotis* with an account of the components of his altar. Or if Herbert's intention was not so pointed, the fact remains that he devised a consecration of an object derived from antiquity for his first church object. Viewing it as such, the modern reader will find certain of its phrases richer in meaning than he might have suspected. The opening lines, a moving paraphrase of two verses of the *Miserere Mei,* suggest as well the rearing of a Christian, not a classical, edifice; *To praise thy Name* reminds one of the different objects of praise of other altar poems; and the concluding couplet, surely, pleads not merely for the blessing of Herbert's poem, but for the sanctification of a normally profane object. *The Altar,* then, is no mere quaint vagary of a naive sensibility, as for two centuries it was mistakenly thought to be, or even an eccentricity redeemed by its skillful combination of Biblical allusions, but rather its maker's declaration of God's ability to turn all of experience, even pagan tradition, to His own.

Herbert's poem, like the previous patterned altars of English writers, concludes with a mention of the kind of sacrifice to be offered there. It is, of course, followed by *The Sacrifice,* in which Christ poignantly arraigns the Jews for their ingratitude over His offering of Himself. It is a mistake, I feel, to regard these two poems as the counterparts of the church altar and the sacrament of Holy

Communion. For Herbert, the Eucharist never suggested a reenactment of the Passion. Following the mode of his fellow churchmen, he regularly characterized this sacrament as the one affording spiritual nourishment for the Christian, providing the most immediate possible communication between him and Christ. For him it memorialized the Passion, but did not recreate it.[22] I suggest that *The Altar* and *The Sacrifice*, representing, as they do, ideas foreign to those in Herbert's identifiable meditations about the sacrament of Holy Communion, are primarily designed to purvey the Christian substitute for pagan and Hebrew sacrificial customs, not (as they are commonly thought to do) to stand as treatments of the Anglican sacrament which takes place upon what Herbert would have called a communion table. Inferior religions require sacrifices for the appeasement of their gods; that which Herbert celebrates can claim a loving God who offered Himself as Sacrifice for His worshippers. To remind the reader of this is, I think, the function of these opening pages of *The Temple*.

Herbert predicates a number of other whole poems upon the contrast between what classical cults could do for their adherents and what God does for His creatures. *The Pulley* is, as several modern commentators have observed, an adaptation of the Pandora story. Whether Herbert meant the reader to think of a late version of the myth, as Hutchinson proposes, and so to conceive man's counterpart as a Pandora given a jar of blessings which escape her, or whether he wished Hesiod's formularization to be the starting point, and so for the jar to contain troubles sent by Jove, is not entirely clear. But the differing details of variant tellings of the story do not cloud the argument of this poem. Clearly, Herbert shows the superiority of God's care for His people to that of classical figures for their subjects, contrasting Jupiter's poverty of provision with God's bounty:

> When God at first made man,
> Having a glasse of blessings standing by;
> Let us (said he) poure on him all we can:
> Let the worlds riches, which dispersed lie,
>   Contract into a span.   (159)

Pandora, after she opens the jar (or, as in some versions, after Epimetheus does so) is left only with hope, whereas God liberally *pours* the delights of the universe on His creatures. Doubtless Herbert's readers would have recognized in God's action the paraphrase of Malachi 3:10: "Prove me now herewith, saith the Lord of hosts, if I will not open you the windows of heaven, and pour you out a blessing, that there shall not be room enough to receive it." The Scriptural allusion is eminently appropriate here, for Herbert undoubtedly presumed that his audience would make the then familiar association of Pandora and Eve: Pandora as first mortal woman loosed troubles into the world, as did Eve. As early as the time of Tertullian, Pandora was felt to prefigure Eve: "Pandora, quam primam feminarum memorat Hesiodus. . . . Nobis vero Moyses propheticus, non poeticus pastor, principem feminam Evam . . . describit."[23] (*Trans.* Hesiod calls Pandora the first of women . . . but Moses, a prophet rather than a poetic shepherd, has truly represented Eve to us as the first woman.) In Herbert's own time, the coupling of the two figures persisted. Robert Stephanus, in his *Thesaurus Linguae Latinae* (1531 and following), offers the following interpretation of Pandora: "Pandora . . . Hesiodo fingitur prima mulier, a Vulcano Iovis iussu fabricata, quam singuli dij donis suis ornaverunt. . . . Hanc postea cum pyxide clausa missam fuisse tradunt ad Epimethum . . . qui illa recepta, & pyxide aperta, cui omne malorum genus inerat, terram morbis calamitatibusque repleuit."[24] (*Trans.* Pandora is imagined the first woman by Hesiod, made by Vulcan at the command of Jove, whom they [the gods]

adorned with gifts. . . . Afterwards they sent her a closed
box by Epimetheus, which she received and opened, in
which was contained the whole race of evils, and which
supplied the earth with diseases and misfortunes.) One
finds the association in Milton. In *The Doctrine and
Discipline of Divorce* Eve is characterized as "a most consummate and most adorned Pandora." And in *Paradise
Lost,* the first woman is revealed on her wedding day "In
naked beauty more adorned, / More lovely than Pandora.
. . ." (IV, 313-14)

The first line of *The Pulley,* then, suggests both the
classical and Biblical versions of the creation of man. And
the God of the Old Testament, speaking in almost the very
words of the prophet Malachi, does supply pre-Messianic
mankind with all worldly riches. Herbert catalogues them
in the second stanza:

> So strength first made a way;
> Then beautie flow'd, then wisdome, honour, pleasure:
> When almost all was out, God made a stay,
> Perceiving that alone of all his treasure
> Rest in the bottom lay.

Rest, however, is a New Testament blessing, one promised
only through the Covenant of Grace. Herbert has the
Creator wisely foresee that all men will not choose good,
in spite of their ampleness of opportunity, and that the
most comfortable of His gifts must be reserved. The poem
ends with God's statement of this reservation framed to
remind the reader of Christ's promise of rest, the Author-
ized Version rendering of Matthew 11:28, the first of the
Comfortable Words of the Order for Holy Communion:

> Yet let him keep the rest [of the world's riches]
> But keep them with repining restlesnesse:
> Let him be rich and wearie, that at least,
> If goodnesse leads him not, yet wearinesse
> May tosse him to my breast.[25]

and mends eyes, that, in the words of Isaiah 33:17, "Thine eyes shall see the king in his beauty: they shall behold the land that is very far off."

In *Vertue*, Herbert brilliantly adapts the materials of the *carpe diem* tradition so that they constitute an argument for purity of soul, rather than for enjoyment of immediate physical pleasure. In structure, the poem is strongly, and probably designedly, reminiscent of the English sonnet, so many specimens of which were written in service of the theme which Herbert here inverts. The first three quatrains, firmly paralleled, are countered by a fourth which functions much like a concluding couplet:

> Sweet day, so cool, so calm, so bright,
> The bridall of the earth and skie:
> The dew shall weep thy fall to night;
> > For thou must die.
>
> Sweet rose, whose hue angrie and brave
> Bids the rash gazer wipe his eye:
> Thy root is ever in its grave,
> > And thou must die.
>
> Sweet spring, full of sweet dayes and roses,
> A box where sweets compacted lie;
> My musick shows ye have your closes,
> > And all must die.
>
> Onely a sweet and vertuous soul,
> Like season'd timber, never gives;
> But though the whole world turn to coal,
> > Then chiefly lives.   (87-88)

Almost every phrase in the first three strophes seems familiar, so close is each to the stock comparisons of the poets who for centuries had sung of the brevity of feminine beauty. In countless seduction poems ladies are warned that their loveliness will fade like the rose, vanish like the brightness of the day, turn, like spring, to the winter of old age. And though Herbert does not pointedly make mention of the human body at all or specify it as medium of physical love, he takes care that the reader thinks of these things throughout. The day is the *bridall* of the earth and sky; the rose is, after all, the timeless symbol of human love; and spring has always been the season of the year appropriated by lovers. Underlying the first twelve lines, then, is one of the most ancient traditions of erotic verse. The very insistence of this theme gives the last stanza its peculiar power. For the introduction of the soul upsets the entire well-realized effect of the foregoing lines. The soul has not only permanence, but permanent sweetness. Beauty of the body is thus disparaged, though not condemned. The success of this little homily depends largely upon the poet's engaging our attention throughout the first strophes on almost false terms: we are surprised and impressed with the praise of the soul only because we have recognized the affinity of the opening lines with conventional celebrations of physical beauty and love.

Several years ago A. Davenport suggested that in *Vertue* Herbert reworked a section of the second book of the *Ars Amatoria,* where one does indeed find many of the elements of the later poem:

> Ut dominam teneas . . .
>   ingenii dotes corporis adde bonis.
> forma bonum fragile est, quantumque accedit ad annos,
>   fit minor et spatio carpitur ipsa suo.
> Nec violae semper nec hiantia lilia florent,
>   et riget amissa spina relicta rosa;
> et tibi iam uenient cani, formose, capilli,
>   iam uenient rugae, quae tibi corpus arent.
> Iam molire animum, qui durent, et adstrue formae:
>   solus ad extremos permanet ille rogos. (II, 111-20)[26]

Trans. That you may keep the lady, combine endowments of character with the goods of the body. A good appearance is fragile, and yields to the years. It diminishes and is plucked from its own space, and the neglected rose stiffens on the thorn; and presently white hairs will come gradually to you, wrinkles will come, which will plow your flesh. Then bestir the soul, which will endure, and add it to the body: it alone finally survives the funeral pyre.

Perhaps this is Herbert's source. Certainly the idea and even some of the expressions of the last two lines closely resemble the final strophe of "Vertue," and Ovid's funeral pyre and *ad extremos* might well have prompted Herbert's allusion to the Last Judgment. In any case, whether adapted from this passage specifically or indebted to the *carpe diem* tradition in general, "Vertue" achieves its ends because of the apparentness of the debt.

In Book XI of the *Metamorphoses,* Ovid tells us that Juno sends Iris to the cave of Sleep to get a dream-vision of the dead Ceyx so that Alcione can learn of her fate. When Iris confronts the god, she addresses a prayer to him: "Somne, quies rerum, placidissime, Somne, deorum, / pax animi, quem cura fugit, qui corpora duris / fessa ministeriis mulces reparasque labori. . . ." (lines 623-25) (*Trans.* O Sleep, the repose of all things, gentlest of the gods, peace of the soul, whom care flees, who softens the hard tasks of tired bodies and refreshes us for labor. . . .) Imitations of these lines provided a stock item for Elizabethan sonnet sequences, where the despairing lover apostrophized sleep as brother to death and praised its soft couch, its welcome darkness, its visions of the beloved, its ability to soothe away the torments of the day. More frequently than not, the pieces ended with the expression of a wish for death.[27] In *Sunday,* Herbert relies upon the reader's familiarity with this convention to show the Lord's day as the true care-charmer and rest for the weary:

> O Day most calm, most bright,
> The fruit of this, the next worlds bud,

> Th' indorsement of supreme delight,
> Writ by a friend, and with his bloud;
> The couch of time; cares balm and bay:
> The week were dark, but for thy light:
>   Thy torch doth show the way.   (75)

But although Sunday affords the chief comforts of sleep—it is *the couch of time, cares balm and bay*—in many ways, as Herbert points out, the two are antithetical, the contrast always working in favor of the former. Sunday is a day of rest, but also of mirth, as we learn in the final stanza. And while the darkness of sleep is but a temporary escape from the unrequited love of daylight, the light of Sunday suffuses the whole week. The nature of this light is indicated in the multi-leveled punning of the title: Herbert lauds a day, rather than an accompaniment of night, and so it is illuminated by the sun; yet though ordinary days derive their light from the solar body, the first day of the week is brightened by the Son, as Herbert comments in the sixth stanza: "This day my Saviour rose, / And did inclose this light for his. . . ." Unlike sleep, then, Sunday can boast both spiritual and natural light. It also gives a real glimpse of Divine Love, rather than dreams of an indifferent mistress:

> Man had straight forward gone
> To endlesse death: but thou dost pull
> And turn us round to look on one,
> Whom, if we were not very dull,
> We could not choose but look on still. . . .

And most important, as we learn in the last lines, the poet values Sunday not as a forerunner of death, but of eternal life:

> O let me take thee at the bound,
> Leaping with thee from sev'n to sev'n,
> Till that we both, being toss'd from earth,
>   Flie hand in hand to heav'n!

Jordan (II), more-than-average disagreement as to its mean-ing persists. Some time ago Grosart suggested an interpreta-tion of the title which still, I feel, holds its own among subsequent proposals. When Herbert named the poem, Grosart said, "It seems plain that he had a double thought: (a) That he was crossing into the Promised Land; (b) That thereupon Jordan was to be his Helicon—the Lord, not the Nine Muses, the source of his inspiration."[32] More recently Blakemore Evans has supported this view, pointing out two seventeenth-century compliments to Herbert which assume the very substitution for which Grosart argued.[33] First, in the prefatory material to the second edition of Christopher Harvey's *The Synagogue* (1647), J. L. wrote that one emulating Herbert

> Must climbe Mount *Calvary* for *Parnassus* Hill,
> And in his Saviours sides baptize his Quill;
> > A Jordan fit t' instill
> A Saint-like stile, backt with an Angel's skill.   (Sig C8)

And second, in the tenth edition of *The Temple* an anonymous versifier bade the reader

> Bring Wreaths of Larick, an immortal Tree,
> To *Salem's* sacred Hill, for Obsequie.
> Parnassus *Mount was never so divine*
> *To turn the Muses Water into Wine.* . . .
> A lasting Spring of Blood Springs near that Hill,
> There he did bathe; there you your Vials fill.   (Sigs A5-6)

Evans might well have mentioned the comments by the printer of the same edition, which almost duplicate the sentiment: "The Dedication of this Work having been made by the Author to the *Divine Majesty* only, how should we presume to interest any mortal man in the patronage of it? Much less think we it meet to seek recommendation of the Muses, for that which himself was confident to have been inspired by a diviner breath than flows from Helicon." (p. *2)

If Herbert intended to specify Jordan rather than
Helicon as his animating force, then the subject of his
attack in the poem must be a kind of verse usually pur-
porting reliance upon the Muses, some sort of quasi-classical
love poetry. This need not, as Rosamund Tuve has made
clear, be all love poetry; rather she feels that Herbert is
objecting to an attitude to profane verse, not to its existence: "*Jordan* (I) is not a protest against love poetry but
against its usurpation of the whole field and very title of
poetry."[34] Nor is his objection likely to be, as Florence
Brinkley claims in her gloss of *Jordan* (II), to the "metaphysical style";[35] at the time when Herbert wrote the
Jordan poems (before 1629), that style was represented in
love poetry almost solely by Donne's unpublished songs,
which, though greatly admired, would scarcely have pro-
voked the charge of fictions *only* and false hair becoming
poetry. Herbert felt, of course, that all love songs were
intrinsically subordinate in importance to divine poetry:
love of God was for him the highest possible theme for the
lyrist. But his quarrel here, it seems to me, is with glib,
cliché-ridden amorous verse, prompted not by genuine sentiment, but by the desire to imitate other imitations—a kind
of writing clogged with useless artificiality and wornout
embellishment, representing the exercise of wit for its own
sake. He does not, we learn in line eight, reproach versifiers
for writing about love, but for plaguing him with an
affection so superficially felt and described that they must
fill in their lines with verbal padding like *purling streams*
and *sudden arbours*. The eye of such rhymesters was not
on nature, or on a real woman, but on other poetic syn-
theses of true objects. Thus the reader must catch the
sense of such verses (and surely here, as elsewhere, Herbert
has in mind both their meaning and their intended sensuous appeal) at two removes.

This charge, needless to say, is not original with
Herbert. It is one of Sidney's familiar burdens; and Herbert
seems not only to echo Sidney's general sentiment but to

have recalled two of his specific treatments of such second-hand productions. One is from the *Defence*:

. . . How well it might be employed, and with how heavenly fruits both private and public, in singing the praises of the immortal beauty, the immortal goodness of that God who giveth us hands to write, and wits to conceive! . . . But truly, many of such writings as come under the banner of unresistible love, if I were a mistress would never persuade me they were in love; so coldly they apply fiery speeches, as man that had rather read lovers' writings, and so caught up certain swelling phrases. . . . Now for the outside of it, which is words, or (as I may term it) diction, it is even well worse, so is that honey-flowing matron eloquence apparelled, or rather disguised, in a courtesan-like painted affection. . . .[36]

Here, as in *Jordan* (I), is the comparison of the praise of God and the feigned admiration of a mistress, a painted affectation limned largely from other artificial writings. Herbert's poem is also reminiscent, I believe, of the fifteenth sonnet in *Astrophel and Stella,* where the dishonesty of imagerial poaching might well have suggested Herbert's honest shepherds and their heartfelt song:

You that do search for everie purling spring,
    Which from the ribs of old *Parnassus* flowes,
    And everie floure, not sweet perhaps, which growes
    Neare therabouts, into your Poesie wring.

You that do Dictionaries methods bring
    Into your rimes, running in ratling rowes:
    You that poore *Petrarchs* long deceased woes,
    With new-borne signes and denisend wit do sing.

You take wrong waies: those far-fet helpes be such,
    As do bewray a want of inward tuch:
    And sure at length stolne goods do come to light.[37]

Herbert conducts his denunciation, however, along more specifically classical lines than Sidney's. *Painted* in *Jordan*

(I), as in Sidney's *Defence,* and as elsewhere in *The Temple,*
denotes unattractive artifice (Herbert cites the Roman
church, for example, as painted). And yet in the Jordan
poem it, and *catching the sense at two removes,* have more
explicit meanings, referring possibly to Plato's discussion in
The Republic X.597-98 of the various removes from truth.
As everyone will remember, Socrates explains to Glaucon
that there are three kinds of beds and three makers of beds:
the true idea of the bed, made by God; the artifact, made
by a carpenter in imitation of the idea; and the painted
bed made by a painter in imitation of what the carpenter
makes. The work of this painter, as well as that of his
fellow imitator, the poet, is far from truth:

> But would you call the painter a creator and maker?
> Certainly not.
> Yet if he is not the maker, what is he in relation to the
> bed?
> I think, he said, that we may fairly designate him as the
> imitator of that which the others make.
> Good, I said; then you call him who is third in the
> descent from nature an imitator?
> Certainly, he said.
> And the tragic poet is an imitator, and therefore, like all
> other imitators, he is thrice removed from the king and
> from the truth?
> That appears to be so.[38]

Drawing upon this famous illustration of imitation, then,
Herbert arraigns the poetic copyists of his own time. All
poets whose inspiration derives from Helicon, who write of
human love, have chosen a subject removed from the truth,
which is God Himself; but those who, like the painter,
imitate what other people have made, have become even
more involved with fiction and falsity. For Herbert, whose
wellspring is Jordan, and who will try to write of truth, not
fable, the most beautiful words are *My God, My King.*

Two other pronouncements of Herbert's lend strong

support to this reading. The concluding piece of the
Passio Discerpta, In Mundi sympathiam cum Christo, specifically names Christ as the revealed world spirit spoken
of by Plato: "Hunc ponas animam mundi, Plato: vel tua
Mundum / Ne nimium vexet quaestio, pone meam." (409)
(Trans. You propose a world-soul, Plato; assuredly your
investigation will not greatly trouble the world: propose
mine [Christ].) And in *Dulnesse,* Herbert with equal specificity cites Christ as the original of love and beauty, earthly
mistresses being mere copies of His form:

> The wanton lover in a curious strain
>   Can praise his fairest fair;
> And with quaint metaphors her curled hair
>   Curl o're again.
>
> Thou are my lovelinesse, my life, my light,
>   Beautie alone to me:
> Thy bloudy death and underserv'd, makes thee
>   Pure red and white.
>
> When all perfections as but one appeare,
>   That those thy form doth show,
> The very dust, where thou dost tread and go,
>   Makes beauties here. (115)

Christ is the pure object of love: human mistresses actually
loved are projections of His form. And fictional mistresses
only feignedly loved are, I think, the subject of the verses
so sharply trounced in *Jordan* (I).

In *Heaven,* the penultimate poem in "The Church,"
Herbert chooses a Greek form, the echo lyric, for his central
dramatic device. Like the shaped verses, the echo would
have seemed "classical" to seventeenth-century readers. Elbridge Colby's excellent account of the type leaves little
doubt of its connotations.[39] It first reached the attention
of the Elizabethan audience through a poem by Gauradas
in, again, the *Greek Anthology.* Imitations followed rapidly.
Among the surviving printed versions are poems by Gas-

coigne in *The Princely Pleasures of Kenilworth Castle*
(1575); Peele in *The Arraignment of Paris* (1584); Sidney
in *The Countess of Pembroke's Arcadia* (1590); Thomas
Watson in *The Teares of Fancy* (1593) and *Hekatompathia*
(1581); William Percy in *Coelia* (1594); Ben Jonson in *A
Masque of Oberon, The Maid's Metamorphosis, Pan's Anniversary,* and *Cynthia's Revels* (1600). The echo poem,
then, one in which questions are answered by repetitions of
their own last syllable or syllables, enjoyed a considerable
vogue by the time of the publication of *The Temple.* My
concern here is that each of these echoes consists of dialogue
between classical personages—including either the figure
Echo popularized by Ovid, or English pastoral figures
consciously reminiscent of classical models. A substantial
ingredient of the pleasure afforded by Herbert's poem, then,
must have been surprise at the bold enlistment of a
conventionally Greek or neo-Greek form for the description
of a Christian heaven.

A possible precedent for this innovation may be found
in the magnificent *Echo in a Church* of Lord Herbert's,
which C. G. Moore Smith places "before 1631."[40] Here the
dialogue takes place between a human supplicant and an
echo which, in the final lines, identifies itself by mentioning
the Old Testament sacred name of God:

> Then quickly speak,
> Since now with crying I am grown so weak
> I shall want force even to crave thy name;
> O speak before I wholly weary am.
> > *Echo.* I am.[41]

If the poem were composed long before Smith's proposed
date, George Herbert might be reasonably expected to have
seen it and so from it to have conceived the idea for his
work. Or perhaps *Heaven* antedates *Echo in a Church.* In
any case, Lord Herbert's verse was not published until
long after the first edition of *The Temple,* and so the echo
poem there would have seemed a real novelty, unless the

Baron's poetry circulated in manuscript more widely than it is possible to imagine.

In *Heaven,* the device is made to work to superb advantage. One might quarrel with Edward Herbert's dramatizing God as an echo of man, although the answers of the voice are impressive enough. But George Herbert allows no such troubles to arise. His questioner initially mistakes the echo for a mere human voice, only to be informed that no such thing is true; but rather that it is the Holy Scriptures, the earthly echo of Heaven:

> O who will show me those delights on high?
> *Echo.*　　I.
> Thou Echo, thou art mortall, all men know.
> *Echo.*　　No.
> Wert thou not born among the trees and leaves?
> *Echo.*　　Leaves.
> And are there any leaves, that still abide?
> *Echo.*　　Bide.
> What leaves are they? impart the matter wholly.
> *Echo.*　　Holy.
> Are holy leaves the Echo then of blisse?
> *Echo.*　　Yes.
> Then tell me, what is that supreme delight?
> *Echo.*　　Light.
> Light to the minde: what shall the will enjoy?
> *Echo.*　　Joy.
> But are there cares and businesse with the pleasure?
> *Echo.*　　Leisure.
> Light, joy, and leisure; but shall they persever?
> *Echo.*　　Ever. (188)

Herbert seems at pains to keep the echo from being the bare phonetic device that it is in many of this poem's generic forerunners. Throughout it is invested with genuine identity, with wisdom, as befits an emissary of Paradise. One way in which this is accomplished is through Herbert's reminder, in lines three and five, of the classical Echo, who lived among trees and leaves. Yet the fact remains that, though as a representative of Heaven, the voice is wiser than the speaker, it *does* echo the human personage of the poem; and appropriately so, for the Bible, as Herbert has elsewhere said, is God's explanation to men of Himself through human exempla. By reading about other people in the Scriptures, man can learn of God and of His dwelling place. See the strikingly similar statement in *The H. Scriptures*:

> . . . This is the thankfull glasse,
> That mends the lookers eyes: this is the well
> That washes what it shows. Who can indeare
> Thy praise too much? thou art heav'ns Lidger here,
> Working against the states of death and hell. (58)

By the very employment of the echo-as-Bible identification, Herbert implies an exact idea of doubleness. When one looks in a glass he sees himself, or an image of himself, just as he finds types of himself in the leaves of Holy Writ, Heaven's Lidger or ambassador.

The concept of Echo as a virtue was not Herbert's invention, nor, if his brother's poem came first, was it Lord Herbert's idea. Echo's story in *Ovide Moralisée* is interpreted in a fashion which may well have prompted the allegory of *Heaven*: the moralizer adopts the conventional equation of Narcissus with pride, but makes Echo into *bonne renommée,* a quality closely akin to the Bible. She, as good or true words, is abused by Juno, or worldliness.[42] And in a similar vein, Ben Jonson has the Echo of his *Cynthia's Revels* identify herself with truth—a more nearly perfect image of truth than Narcissus found reflected in the water. Echo as true mirror closely resembles the glass in *The H. Scriptures* and the leaves of Holy Writ in *Heaven*. Herbert seems, then, to have drawn upon and combined two separate Echo traditions—one of the character's connotations, the other of the lyric device.

Love (III), the next poem, concludes "The Church."

As Joseph Summers has so convincingly argued, the banquet of which it speaks is not the earthly Communion, the sacrament of the Church, but the final Communion in Heaven, for which the Church prepares us, the one spoken of in Luke 12:37: "He shall gird himselfe, and make them to sit down to meat, and will come forth and serve them." Like *Love* (I) and *Love* (II), it tacitly compares the immortal love of the Figure welcoming the soul to Heaven with the more transient and selfish passions inspired by Cupid. Even more fully than in *Love* (II), Herbert in this final poem celebrates the superiority of Divine Love to blind Cupid in that the greater Love is both seeing and wise, and also creates vision, and consequently, acumen, in His adherents: this Love is not blind, but rather a revealer of light:

> Love bade me welcome: yet my soul drew back,
> > Guiltie of dust and sinne.
> But quick-ey'd Love, observing me grow slack
> > From my first entrance in,
> Drew nearer to me, sweetly questioning,
> > If I lacked any thing.
>
> A guest, I answer'd worthy to be here:
> > Love said, You shall be he.
> I, the unkinde, ungratefull? Ah my deare,
> > I cannot look on thee.
> Love took my hand, and smiling did reply,
> > Who made the eyes but I? (188-89)

It is, then, as Herbert has said in *The Pearl,* not seeled but with open eyes that the beloved is served by Love:

> Truth, Lord, but I have marr'd them: let my shame
> > God where it doth deserve.
> And know you not, sayes Love, who bore the blame?
> > My deare, then I will serve.
> You must sit down, sayes Love, and taste my meat:
> > So I did sit and eat.

An appreciable number of the items of *The Temple,*
as we have seen, are pervaded by a contrast between the
life of grace offered by the Church and the natural values
of the ancients. This disparity forms the central motif of
*The Church-porch, Superliminare, The Altar, Easter-wings,
Love* (I) and (II), *Jordan* (I), *Humilitie, Sunday, Vertue,
Time, The Pulley, The Rose, A Wreath, Heaven,* and *Love*
(III). Yet one has only begun to assess Herbert's adaptations of Greek and Roman materials when he has considered these poems. Dozens of others include passing
references to poets, mythological figures, and classical customs, references no less telling because of their brevity. In
a number, one finds the comparison of the loves inspired
by God and Cupid, the contrast afforded by *Love* (I) and
Love (II). In *The Temper* (II), *Artillerie,* and *Longing,*
Herbert mentions the darts of Divine Love; in *Even-song,*
he contrasts the sight given by the God of love with Cupid's
blindness; in *The Invitation,* he invites to God's table all
who live under the domination of Venus's doves; in *Miserie*
and *Grieve not the Holy Spirit,* the Holy Ghost, God's
"milde Dove," is paralleled with those of the goddess of
beauty; in *The Thanksgiving, Grace,* and *Mattens,* he refers
to God's art of love. Christ as Divine Cupid, then, figures
repeatedly in *The Temple.*

I might pause briefly over the most famous poem
embodying this motif, since here the rather unusual character of the Divine Lover brings the entire argument into
focus. *Discipline* is far more than a platitudinous plea for
the replacement of justice by mercy; and although Herbert
asks for God's wrath with him to be set aside in favor of
the love of Christ, he does not request a foregoing of all
discipline. Man has frailties, as he concludes, which must
be controlled; and Christ, who, far more effectually than
Cupid, relentlessly hunts and can hit from afar, is the
perfect agent for this control:

Then let wrath remove;
Love will do the deed:
        For with love
Stonie hearts will bleed.

Love is swift of foot;
Love's a man of warre,
        And can shoot,
And can hit from farre.

Who can scape his bow?
That which wrought on thee,
        Brought thee low,
Needs must work on me. (179)

Christ as Divine Love exercises powers far beyond those possessed by Cupid: even the godhead has been lowered to the level of man by His bow. Surely Herbert must have thought of the passage in the Apocalypse commonly used as authority for the identification of Christ with Divine Cupid:[43]

And I saw heaven opened, and behold a white horse; and he that sat upon him was called Faithful and True, and in righteousness doth judge and make war. His eyes were as a flame of fire, and on his head were many crowns; and he had a name written, that no man knew, but he himself. And he was clothed in a vesture dipped in blood: and his name is called the Word of God. And the armies which were in heaven followed him upon white horses, clothed in fine linen, white and clean. And out of his mouth goeth a sharp sword, that with it he should smite the nations: and he shall rule them with a rod of iron: and he treadeth the winepress of the fierceness and wrath of Almighty God. And he hath on his vesture and on his thigh a name written, KING OF KINGS AND LORD OF LORDS. (Revelation 19:11-16)

The very power of this figure gives *Discipline* its point. For as Herbert makes clear, his petition is not for God's wrath to be supplanted by a lax and indulgent Love, but by

One almost more potent and mighty than it is possible to imagine. Yet He will remove wrath; He will both discipline by making the stony heart to bleed and do the deed of taking away the winepress of God's wrath. This is the Discipliner whom Herbert invokes.

Thumbing through *The Temple,* one finds far more varied and more original transformations of classical motif than the conventional one of the Christianized Cupid. In *The Church-porch,* Herbert ranges through considerable ancient territory. In the first stanza, he explains that his purpose is to instruct while delighting: "Hearken unto a Verser, who may chance / Ryme thee to good, and make a bait of pleasure." (6) Lowe recognized this period as an inversion of one of Cicero's sayings: "Divine Plato escam malorum appelat voluptatem."[44] (*Trans.* Plato admirably terms pleasure the bait of evil.)

When he urges temperance, Herbert uses several classical analogies in *The Church-porch.* "Drink not the third glasse," he says in the fifth stanza. Hutchinson cites this line as a paraphrase of Panyasis.[45] In stanza eight, he makes the almost standard comparison of drunkenness and the metamorphosis wrought by Circe on Odysseus' men:

> If reason move not Gallants, quit the room,
> (All in a shipwrack shift their severall way)
> Let not a common ruine thee intombe:
> Be not a beast in courtesie; but stay,
>   Stay at the third cup. . . . (8)

Twice he uses the metaphor of the sensuous man as a driver of a vehicle drawn by unmanageable horses:

> He that is drunken, may his mother kill
> Bigge with his sister: he hath lost the reins,
> Is outlawd by himself. . . . (7)

> Be not thine own worm: yet such jealousie,
> As hurts not others, but may make thee better,

Is a good spurre. Correct thy passions spite:
Then may the beasts draw thee to happy light. (16)

This figure derives ultimately from *Phaedrus* 253-54, where
Plato describes the soul of a god as a driver drawn by two
winged horses upward to heavenly light, the soul of the
mortal as a charioteer using earthly horses, striving to move
toward a beloved god, but hampered by the unruliness of
one of his animals, which not yielding to whip and spur,
causes his master to drop the reins. Although the allegory
was commonly alluded to in Herbert's day, Plato's fable
alone explains all of the details in *The Church-porch*
passages. Since the charioteer and horses are components
of the same soul, the driver who has lost the reins is truly
hindered by himself, or a part of himself; and only with
the punishment of the passionate horse can the reason use
the affections to arrive at a goal of happy light.

Another section of *The Church-porch* is devoted to
maxims governing the education of youth. Herbert advo-
cates encouraging tranquillity: "For wealth without contentment climbes a hill / To feel these tempests, which fly
over ditches." (11) Grosart saw these lines as an adaptation
from Horace: "Saepius ventis agitur ingens / Pinus; et
celsae graviore casu / Decidunt turres, feriuntque summos /
Fulgura montes."[46] (*Trans.* More frequently the huge pine
is shaken by the winds; and lofty towers fall ever more
heavily; and thunderbolts batter the highest mountains.)
Later in the poem Herbert refers to Aesop's fable of the
ass carrying an image on its back:

When basenesse is exalted, do not bate
The place its honour, for the persons sake.
The shrine is that which thou dost venerate,
And not the beast, that bears it on his back.[47]

Still later, as Lowe noticed, he paraphrases Cicero's "Deinde,
ne maior benignitas sit, quam facultates: tum, ut pro digni-

tate cuique tribuatur"[48] (*Trans.* Therefore let not benevo-
lence be greater than means: and then let it be given
according to merit), rendering it: "In Almes regard thy
means, and other merit." He concludes *The Church-porch*
with a couplet summarizing the effects of good and evil
conduct: "If thou do ill; the joy fades, not the pains: / If
well; the pain doth fade, the joy remains." (24) These
lines have, as Hutchinson comments (p. 483), a long literary
history. Aulus Gellius quotes them from a speech of Cato
the Censor at Numidia, 195 B.C.; other Greek versions
became associated with later philosophers, to be printed in
several sixteenth-century English books, including one by
Sir Humphrey Gilbert which Hakluyt reprinted.

Moving on to *The Church,* we find Herbert has the
Christ of the Sacrifice comment on the folly of his betrayers
approaching Him to make the arrest:

> Arise, arise, they come. Look how they runne!
> Alas! that haste they make to be undone!
> How with their lanterns do they seek the sunne! (27)

Perhaps he meant us to associate the observation of the
last line with the famous story of Diogenes carrying a
lantern in broad daylight in search of a true man, a story
popularized in sixteenth-century emblem books.[49] The
allusion intensifies the soldiers' vanity. Unknowingly they
have found the truest of men, the One Who would have
satisfied even the Cynic. Yet Herbert renders their search
even more absurd by making them look for the overwhelmingly evident sun (with a significant pun on *Son*)
with the gratuitous aid of their puny individual lights.
Their spiritual blindness is perceived in counterpoint to
Diogenes' earnest quest.

In several lines of *Prayer* (I), Herbert draws upon
classical materials for his analysis of this Christian phenomenon. Surely the *Engine against th' Almightie* and
Reversed thunder of the second quatrain are designed to

remind one of Jupiter the hurler of thunderbolts. For Jupiter's subjects no retaliation was possible. The process was one-sided. They had to be content to suffer whatever punishment the god might hurl down, however capriciously assigned. But the Christian, Herbert shows in this metaphor, is invested by his loving deity with a means of using God's power itself. Through prayer, he can reverse thunder and storm the very throne of Grace—this because it is a throne of Grace, not merely of authority, as is Jupiter's. Christian prayer affords the believer abilities, then, denied the devout ancient, or, if you will, the natural man.

Prayer as *the milkie way* makes a similar differentiation. Jupiter designed the Milky Way, of course, as a pathway to his palace when, incensed by the corruptions of the Iron Age, he summoned the gods to a parley to decide the fate of the world. This Milky Way was, Ovid carefully explains, the prestige street of the heavens:

> Est via sublimis, caelo manifesta sereno,
> Lactea nomen habet; candore notabilis ipso.
> Hac iter est Superis ad magni tecta Tonantis,
> Regalemque domum. Dextra laevaque Deorum
> Atria nobilium valvis celebrantur apertis.
> Plebs habitant diversa locis. (I. 168-73)

Trans. The highroad, clear in the bright sky, is called the Milky Way, extraordinary in brightness. It is the way for the celestial deities to approach the roofs of the great Thunderer, the royal palace. On the left and right are crowded the halls of the gods, their doors open. Commoners live elsewhere.

Herbert's Milky Way corresponds to this one, yet is infinitely better. Like most Renaissance men, he doubtless felt himself to be living in an Iron Age, deeply in need of some cosmic reformation. The Milky Way of prayer enables him to answer God's summons and travel to His presence. The signal disparity of the two highways is revealed, however,

by the fact that *all* Christians are invited to make this
pilgrimage of the heart, all can undergo a kind of deifica-
tion through believing prayer—the doctrine so clearly presented in the Fourth Gospel and the Johannine epistles,
which Herbert used in one other passage in *The Temple,*
in the first stanza of *Ungratefulnesse*:

> Lord, with what bountie and rare clemencie
>   Hast thou redeem'd us from the grave!
>   If thou hadst let us runne,
>   Gladly had man ador'd the sunne,
>   And thought his god most brave;
> Where now we shall be better gods than he.   (82)

By the Milky Way—if one admits *Ungratefulnesse* as gloss
of *Prayer* (I)—any person can become better than the
Jovian deities. The way is open to all.

　　Two other metaphors of *Prayer* (I) were possibly intended by Herbert to suggest classical parallels. One is *A
kinde of tune, which all things heare and fear,* which, following *The six-daies world transposing in an houre,* calls to
mind the music of the spheres. The other is *the bird of
Paradise,* unique in Herbert's verse, which Hutchinson feels
possibly chosen for its name and bright coloring, possibly
to evoke the new world creature which was thought to
reside constantly in the air. This is unlikely, I feel, since
that aerial bird, better known than the editor seems to have
realized, was designated by the compilers of emblem books
as an associate of Fortune, compelled (because of its lack
of feet),[50] to remain hovering in the air and blown about
by the aimless winds, unable to control its course. Surely
Herbert would not have relished suggesting that prayer was
as haphazard as Fortune. The answer to the puzzle lies, I
believe, in the fact that in the seventeenth century the
expression *bird of paradise* was not equated with a definite
species; rather the name was applied to several brightly
colored birds. Skelton speaks in the first lines of *Speke*

Parot of parrots and birds of paradise as synonymous. For Herbert to refer to a parrot in his poem is not as grotesque as one might first think, since in his time it was widely regarded as a symbol of eloquence.[51] But other poets called peacocks and phoenixes birds of paradise,[52] and so conceivably one of these ancient birds is the fowl of the poem. Medieval exegetes took these birds from Greek literature and made the peacock concomitant with immortality (and Renaissance painters frequently depicted peacocks in their renditions of the Nativity), and the phoenix with Christ and the Resurrection.[53] The associative complex of either would enormously enrich *Prayer* (I). Prayer, as Herbert indicates in the poem, enables human beings to transcend ordinary time and space; it is love, both of and by God. Identifying Herbert's bird of paradise with either the phoenix or the peacock, readings with seventeenth-century precedents, would imply both of these concepts.

The Pearl, which has been reprinted as often as any poem in *The Temple,* is "about" what the title implies—the giving up of all that one has in order to purchase the kingdom of Heaven. The all that one has, Herbert describes in the first three stanzas: "I know the wayes of Learning . . . Yet I love thee"; "I know the wayes of Honour . . . Yet I love thee"; "I know the wayes of Pleasure . . . Yet I love thee." It is in the final, and, I think, the most difficult, stanza that Herbert's *attitude* to these ways appears:

> I know all these, and have them in my hand:
> Therefore not sealed, but with open eyes
> I flie to thee, and fully understand
> Both the main sale, and the commodities;
> And at what rate and price I have thy love;
> With all the circumstances that may move:
> Yet through these labyrinths, not my groveling wit,
> But thy silk twist let down from heav'n to me,
> Did both conduct and teach me, how by it
> > To climbe to thee. (89)

By means of three metaphors Herbert shows the inferiority of the ways described in the first stanzas, and at the same time defends their value in informing the persona of the superiority of the route to Heaven. Knowledge of worldly ways, available to him through free will, enables him to fly unseeled to the Falconer and fully to understand the nature and terms of the purchase of the Kingdom. Learning, honor, and pleasure are goodly pearls which, appreciated by the collector, sharpen his awareness of the uniqueness of the pearl of great price. But the third metaphor of the stanza offers the most precise characterization of the three ways, and it is this one with which we must be most concerned here. Herbert introduces the myth of the labyrinth and the twist and thereby shows the futility of pursuing only the three ways: they are but the passages in a maze, winding and leading back upon themselves. The exercise of the poet's groveling wit, the knowing of these ways, leads only to other underground paths. It remains for another kind of knowledge, closely allied with the "Yet I love thee" refrain of the first three stanzas, to show the way upward. Herbert symbolized this love-knowing by the silk twist, an adaptation of the linen thread which Ariadne charitably used to guide Theseus from the labyrinth. Rosamund Tuve has most perceptively glossed the twist: "The image seems to be a combination of *scala coeli* and the clue in the labyrinth; the first more traditional figure, familiarly related to the descent, in the Incarnation, of Christ by whom we climb, would allow the connection with *Love* coming down from heaven to conduct and teach— confirmed by the refrain."[54] Miss Tuve is right, I think. Just as Christ relates the parable of the pearl in the First Gospel, teaching the way to attain the kingdom, He is the silk twist, allowed for a time to walk the mazes of the world, and both by His life and doctrine to lift man to God. Vaughan seems to have accepted this interpretation of the clue, in *Retirement* and *The Knot* directly postulating Christ as a love-twist let down from Heaven.[55]

Coupling the labyrinth myth and the Redemption was not original with Herbert. In *Ovide Moralisée* the story of the Minotaur and Theseus' descent into the labyrinth is allegorized in a manner strongly suggestive of the complex of materials in *The Pearl*. The Minotaur, the poet explains, is of double form, the result of the pride and lust of Pasiphae; because of his evil, Minos had to confine him to a prison:

> Le monstre qui double forme a
> Tel com nature le forma
> Mynos p~le monstre enfremer
> Fut une fort p̃son fremer.[56]

He signifies the devil, the moralist continues, whose monstrous pride and lust for power so angered God that He threw him into an infernal cage, *"orrible et obscure,"* where he lurks ready to corrupt human beings who pass its door. Theseus is a type of Christ, who embarks from Athens on the sea of human life, grapples with the beast, and shows the way out of the labyrinth—an allegory of the Incarnation akin to that of the last stanza of *The Pearl*.

Herbert initiates the ephemeral pageantry of *The World* by assessing the effect of the Roman goddess Fortuna, armed with her wheel:

> Love built a stately house; where *Fortune* came,
> And spinning phansies, she was heard to say,
> That her fine cobwebs did support the frame,
> Whereas they were supported by the same:
> But Wisdome quickly swept them all away. (84)

In *Vanitie* (II), Herbert contrasts two kinds of souls, the aspiring and the earthbound:

Poore silly soul, whose hope and head lies low;
Whose flat delights on earth do creep and grow;
To whom the starres shine not so fair, as eyes;
Nor solid work, as false embroyderies;
Heark and beware, lest what you now do measure
And write for sweet, prove a most sowre displeasure.

    .   .   .   .   .

If souls be made of earthly mold,
    Let them love gold;
    If born on high,
Let them unto their kindred flie:
For they can never be at rest,
Till they regain their ancient nest. (111)

The main concern is, of course, the vanity of adoring the creation instead of the Creator and so of losing the desire for the Kingdom of Heaven. But Herbert dramatizes the vanity in terms of Plato's two orders of souls, described by Socrates in the *Phaedrus* 248-51. Base souls, he explains, after their incarnation at birth forget their former heavenly existence, and, sinking beneath the double load of forgetfulness and vice, lose their wings and drop to the ground (248). But the pure soul, whose recollection persists throughout his life, "forgets earthly interests and is rapt in the divine . . . transported with the recollection of true beauty; he would like to fly away, but he cannot; he is like a bird fluttering and looking upward and careless of the world below . . ." (249). Whereas Plato appears to feel that each human being is moved involuntarily by the predetermined nature of his soul, Herbert, in his Christian adaptation of the myth, ascribes to man free will and the accompanying ability to fix his own course:

O heare betimes, lest thy relenting
    May come too late!
To purchase heaven for repenting
    Is no hard rate.

    .   .   .   .   .

> Then silly soul take heed; for earthly joy
> Is but a bubble, and makes thee a boy. (111)

Self-knowledge and repentance, then, can give wings to the Christian soul.

Of similar derivation is the much-admired third stanza of *Death,* in which Herbert describes the view of that inevitability which prevailed before it was transformed by Christ:

> We lookt on this side of thee, shooting short;
>   Where we did finde
>   The shells of fledge souls left behinde,
> Dry dust, which sheds no tears, but may extort. (186)

The figure of the fledge souls is Platonic. In the *Phaedrus* 250-52, Socrates explains that the soul is imprisoned in the living tomb of the body, much like the oyster in its shell. When a human catches a glimpse of the good, his wings begin to sprout and then to grow; and if he is fortunate enough to attain a union with the good, the soul flies from the body. Herbert here uses many of the details of Plato's myth. Before Christ taught man to look on the "soul side" of death and to contemplate the union of the spirit with God in heaven, all that he could see was the shell which the winged and departed soul had left on earth. Since the Resurrection, he concludes, one can look with equal serenity at sleep and death.

Sinnes round contains two classical allusions, the recognition of which helps one to perceive the double course of evil which Herbert attributes to sinfulness. For sin leads its victims around in futile circles, a concept suggested by the interlocking rhymes of the poem *(am, ring, flame, bring, draughts, thoughts; thoughts, Hill, faults, ill, intentions, inventions; inventions, high, dissensions, supplie, shame, am)*; and at the same time it builds a structure three stories high, much like the tower of Babel, we are informed in the last stanza, as offensive thoughts provoke words, and words, deeds—which begin the round anew by suggesting new thoughts of sin. In the first strophe Herbert symbolizes the harm of sinful thoughts:

> My thoughts are working like a busie flame,
> Untill their cockatrice they hatch and bring:
> And when they once have perfected their draughts,
> My words take fire from my inflamed thoughts. (122)

Admittedly the cockatrice was a familiar fixture of Renaissance verse, and was frequently mentioned by authors apparently intending no reference to its classical heritage; but these writers were concerned with only one of the serpent's characteristics—its ability to kill its prey either by its fiery breath or by its deadly glance. Herbert, however, with his insistence on the twofold motion of sin, appears to have in mind Pliny's description of the beast (*Naturalis Historia* VIII. 33), which invests it with the ability to coil, like an ordinary serpent, but also to advance lofty and upright. The Fathers, also apparently remembering the cockatrice of the ancients, associated it with the serpent in Genesis, which evidently approached Eve in an upright position, since after the temptation scene God bade it henceforth to go on its belly. The explanation in the *Glossa Ordinaria* of Isaiah 11:8b, for example ("The weaned child shall put his hand on the cockatrice den"), is that the infant Jesus shall place His hand of divine power on the devil (*Patrologia Latina,* CXIII, 1251). The double nature of the cockatrice (Pliny explains that it comes from a cock's egg hatched by a serpent), as well as its upstanding posture and consequent resemblance to the tempter of the Old Testament, befits it as a symbol of sin, placing it in the company of such creatures as the satyr, the centaur, and the Minotaur. Herbert makes his monster, then, entail duplicity, deadliness, and ambiguity of motion.

The second station of sin's progress is traced in the intermediate stanza of *Sinnes round*:

> My words take fire from my inflamed thoughts,
> Which spit it forth like the Sicilian Hill.
> They vent the wares and passe them with their faults,
> And by their breathing ventilate the ill.
> But words suffice not, where are lewd intentions:
> My hands do joyn to finish the inventions.

Herbert moves the reader from the breathings and meanderings of the cockatrice to the workshop of the Cyclops, whose destructive wares were, of course, forged beneath Mount Aetna with the benefit of its fires, and then passed on to Jupiter to be used in the throes of his wrath. Herbert's deeds, here, parallel the artisanship of Vulcan's giants.

The second stanza of *Self-condemnation* includes a mythological allusion hitherto overlooked:

> He that doth love, and love amisse,
> This worlds delights before true Christian joy,
> Hath made a Jewish choice:
> The world an ancient murderer is:
> Thousands of souls it hath and doth destroy
> With her enchanting voice. (170)[57]

The last three lines refer to the Sirens, implying two allegorical characteristics for these creatures standard in Renaissance poetry. One is their worldliness. In *Ovide Moralisée* the commentator, glossing *Metamorphoses* XIV. 88, explains that they represent worldly distractions trying to lure Holy Church and to keep it from reaching the true port.[58] The correspondence is so close that Herbert might well have composed this stanza with *Ovide Moralisée* in mind, since he insists in this stanza on the *world's* delights, and on the enchanting voice of the *world,* an ancient murderer. He invests them with another familiar quality,

voluptuousness, or, as he expresses it, loving amiss the
world's delights. Starnes and Talbert[59] have shown the
concurrence of Renaissance classical dictionaries on the
Sirens as symbols of sensual pleasure. Herbert's Sirens,
then, embody both the general notion of worldliness and
the more specific vice of sensuality.

In *The Church-floore* Herbert comments that sometimes sin enters the church (the human heart) and defiles
the marble squares of the floor, "but all is cleansed when
the marble weeps" (67). Hutchinson points out (p. 499)
his probable source in Vergil: "Et maestrum illacrimat
templis ebur, aeraque sudant." (*Geo.* i.480. *Trans.* And
the melancholy ivory of the temple weeps, and the bronzes
sweat.) *Constancie* begins with the question, "Who is the
honest man?" Palmer notes the similarity to Horace's
Integer Vitae, a paraphrase of which had just appeared in
Campion's *The Man of Life Upright.*[60] In *Gratefulnesse,*
the maxim "Much would have more" appears. Hutchinson
cites the source (p. 521) in Horace C. III.xvi.42-43): "Multa
petentibus desunt multa." (*Trans.* Those who desire much
lack much.)

In *The Bag,* Herbert tacitly compares the humble
coming of Christ with the famous appearance of Aeneas:
"He, who came hither all alone, / Bringing nor man, nor
arms, nor fear. . . ." (151)

Stanza three of *The Glimpse* alludes to some ancient
fable:

> Lime begg'd of old, they say,
> A neighbour spring to cool his inward heat;
> Which by the springs accesse grew much more great. (154)

Hutchinson comments on the similarity to No. XXXV of
the *Aenigmata* of Symphosius: "Euasi flammas, ignis tor-
menta profugi: / Ipsa medella meo pugnat contraria fato; /
Infundor lymphis: gelidis incendor ab vndis." (531) (*Trans.*
I have left the flames behind, I have fled the torments of

fire. The contrary remedy itself fights my fate: I am deluged by springs, I am burned by icy waves.)

Justice (II) is customarily read as Herbert's declaration of thankfulness at the displacement of the Old Testament rule of justice by that of mercy. While the statement of this theme is undoubtedly one of the intentions of the poem, some details suggest that the poet also had in mind a comparison of Christ's mercy with the shortcomings of classical arbiters. The first three lines of the third stanza refer to the pronouncement of Hebrews 10:20 that man can now enter into heaven, the Christian holy of holies, "by a new and living way, which he hath consecrated for us, through the vail, that is to say, his flesh":

> But now that Christ's pure vail presents the sight,
> I see no fears:
> Thy hand is white. . . . (141)

Herbert surely wishes us to understand the contrast with the inanimate veil before the holy of holies of the tabernacle, through which only the high priest could pass. But he might also have remembered Homer's account in the *Iliad* 15.185 ff. (repeated and analyzed in the *Gorgias*) of another veil of flesh, the flesh of other judges, which prevented the enactment of fair judgment over the souls of the dead. When Zeus first reigned, he discovered that the destination of man's soul was determined on the day of his death, while he was still alive. All too frequently these determinations were unjust, since the body of the judge veiled or concealed his own soul from the soul of the person being tried. As Zeus says, "The judges are awed by them, and they themselves too have their clothes [their bodies, the garments of the soul] on when judging; their eyes and ears and their whole bodies are interposed as a veil before their own souls." Here is a neat polarity with the veil of Christ's flesh, which, as Herbert points out, does not obstruct but which *presents the sight*.

In the concluding section of *The Temple,* "The Church
Militant," Herbert changes his method of employing the
materials of Greece and Rome. Here he is writing history,
chronicling the birth, spread, and gradual corruption of
organized Christianity, and he is explicit, not suggestive, in
his use of proper names. Within the first lines of the poem,
those dealing with Christian backgrounds and beginnings,
one finds Macarius and Antony, the Sophists, Plato, Aristotle, Alexander, Greek oracles, and the Roman emperors
specifically cited. When the occasion demanded it, then,
Herbert was not averse to an explicit treatment of the
matters to which he so obliquely alludes in the first two
parts of his work.

Yet for the most part, his management of classical
elements departs markedly from Elizabethan precedents.
He varies from other devotional writers in the thoroughness
with which he weaves his allusions into the texture of his
verse, not in the purpose for which he intends them. Using
mythology and ancient philosophy to prove the glory of
God was a standard technique of his day. *Ovide Moralisée*
was taught in the London schools.[61] Fifteenth- and sixteenth-century painters allegorized Greek and Roman figures in their religious work. Composers of emblem books
and Biblical exegetes never wearied of paralleling sacred
incident and ancient myth. Bacon moralized the myths in
De Sapentia Veterum; Raleigh did so in *The History of
the World.* The poets of the moral tradition most widely
circulated in the 1620s—Barnabe Barnes, Giles and Phineas
Fletcher, Spenser, Sylvester, Sir John Davies, Donne, Wither,
and Quarles—to a man broadened the scope of their verse
by the free inclusion of motifs from the ancient world. It
should not prove surprising, then, to find Herbert doing the
same thing. But he does the same thing in a highly
individual manner.

He is even less like the secular poets of his century.
He avoids, for one thing, imposing a window-dressing of

quasi-classicism on his verses by the use of the names of gods and goddesses without meaningful reference to the myths in which they figure—a glibness accounting for a good part of the "classical" gloss of the sonneteers. Unlike many versifiers of his time, Herbert was fully able to refer to the dawn without mentioning Aurora, to mention the sun and moon without abducting Apollo and Diana, to describe tears without benefit of Niobe. He does not affix classical labels to universal phenomena when they are not to be contemplated in a classical context.

Perhaps a more important distinction, however, is Herbert's avoidance in *The Temple* of the proper names of classical figures and landmarks. In this respect he differs even from Donne, who, although in rebellion at the easy veneer of antiquity which decorated much of the verse of his time, in prose and poetry alike felt no compunctions about naming ancient divinities and places. Not so with Herbert. Except in "The Church Militant," where his subject prompts him to list names, in the whole of *The Temple* he uses only a scant handful of classical titles. And in palpable contrast to the italicized nominations of most Renaissance poetry, these are managed so that they stand out as little as possible from their contexts. He mentions Caesar in *The Sacrifice,* but we apprehend him as the personification of government that he is in the Bible, not as a Roman individual; he alludes to the Gordian knot in *Divinitie,* but by using its plural form relieves the specificity of the reference; in *Heaven,* he names Echo, yet her name then, as it is now, was so frequently used as a common noun that it did not operate in sole reference to the Echo-Narcissus-Juno story. These are the only such names in "The Church-porch" and "The Church," despite the fact that almost a third of the poems in these sections depend upon classical materials of some sort or another.

Why was Herbert so careful to avoid specific names? That he did so has meant that many present-day readers

overlook a large body of his reference and so miss a great
deal of the richness of his verse. But manifestly the same
was not true in his own century, when people boasting any
learning at all were familiar with the literature of the
ancients, not half-familiar with the simplifications of mythological dictionaries. For such an audience, Herbert did not
need to name names: his method of alluding to a salient
detail or two of a myth or of paraphrasing a passage from
a Latin author was enough to assure understanding, if not
illumination, among readers of *The Temple*. And indeed,
seventeenth-century evidence shows these readers aware of
Herbert's comparisons between the gods and God. I have
noted in connection with *Jordan* (I) three early comments
on Herbert's exchanging Parnassus for Calvary, turning the
Muses' water into wine, and transforming Helicon into a
baptizing Jordan. Perhaps I might mention one or two
more such observations. Prefacing the tenth edition of
The Temple is an anonymous verse entitled *A Memorial to
the Honorable* GEORGE HERBERT:

> The Graces all, Both Moral and Devine,
> In thee concenter, and with thee combine:
> These Sacred Lessons Set to thy sweet Lute,
> Was Musick that would make Apollo mute:
> Nay, all those warbling Chanters of the Spring,
> Would sit half tame to hear Arion Sing.

In the same edition P. D. also typifies Herbert as outranking
classical poets, apparently on their own grounds:

> You weeping Marbles: *Monuments* we trust,
> As well with the Injurious, as the just.
> When your great trust at last shall be resign'd
> And when his noble dust, shall be refind:
> You shall more Gold, Mirrh, Frankinsence return,
> Than shall be found in great *Augustus* Urn.

In the tenth edition, an engraving faces the *Superliminare,* showing a classical temple with a scutcheon over the door bearing a skull and bones—testimony that the printer recognized the classical substance of that poem (see the frontispiece). The full title of Crashaw's 1646 volume is *Steps to the Temple, Sacred Poems, with other Delights of the Muses*, which, the printer explains to the reader, he felt appropriate for Herbert's second, but equal. Joseph Beaumont compared Herbert favorably with Pindar and Horace, writing that he took their precious metal and cast it in holier molds.[62] These comments imply, I think, not only that Herbert is as good as the ancients and their modern imitators, and therefore worthy of comparison, but that he transformed the components of their verse and fitted them to a Christian theme. He used the Muses' water, though he transformed it; he used the metal of Pindar and Horace, though in another mold. For an audience who could see this, Herbert did not have to explain in *The Pearl* that the world is like a labyrinth at the center of which is the Minotaur of double form, and that God, like Ariadne, helps man, as she did Theseus, to escape from its mazes. All he needed to do was to mention the labyrinth and the silk twist, leaving his reader to assess the implications of the myth for himself.

But surely more than confidence in the cognitive powers of his audience led Herbert to avoid using classical names, for he appears to have made a genuine effort to avoid them. The answer lies, probably, in the very purpose for which he uses classical imagery and motif: the consistent demonstration of the degree to which the happiness of the Christian surpasses that of the pre-Christian, or natural, man and of the contrast between God's total concern for His creatures and the meretricious activities of the deities of the ancients. In the *Love* sonnets, for example, Cupid is not designated by name, and appropriately so, for the poems seek to establish the emptiness and deviousness of the passion which he inspires in comparison with

the afflatus of Immortal Love and Immortal Heat. By
noting his blindness and his descent from beauty, Herbert
takes care that the reader recognizes the little god and
distinguishes him from earthly love in general; but since
the purpose of the argument is to show his inferiority to
Divine Love, he is merely described, while Immortal Love
is explicitly named. Here, as elsewhere, the Christian
member of the parallel is well lighted, whereas the pagan
antithesis remains in shadow. Using every device at his
command, Herbert demonstrates the propriety of subordinating the natural to the divine.

2

Sacred Quibbles

WE HAVE SEEN the ambiguity of *The Temple*'s title and have remarked the number of Herbert's themes which it suggests. And just as it presages more than one subject repeatedly treated in the verse, it also sets the pattern for one of the poet's most important instruments of language, the serious pun.[1] In *The Sonne,* Herbert voices strong approval of verbal ambiguity: his defence of the English tongue rests solidly on the opportunities for punning which it affords:

> Let forrain nations of their language boast,
> What fine varietie each tongue affords:
> I like our language, as our men and coast:
> Who cannot dresse it well, want wit, not words.
> How neatly doe we give one onely name
> To parents issue and the sunnes bright starre!
> A sonne is light and fruit; a fruitfull flame
> Chasing the fathers dimnesse, carri'd farre
> From the first man in th' East, to fresh and new

Western discov'ries of posteritie.
So in one word our Lords humilitie
We turn upon him in a sense most true:
    For what Christ once in humblenesse began,
    We him in glorie call, *The Sonne of Man.* (167-68)

That one word could name a multiplicity of quantities
was a linguistic potentiality which Herbert never allowed
to remain idle, and one which he used in such a distinctive
way that it accounts for an appreciable part of his poetic
effect. Even his commonplace and colloquial words frequently embody concomitant notes of metaphor; a small
word, one like *sun,* can convey several ideas. Herbert's
witty quibbles constitute a weightier component of his
verse than is generally conceded, as I hope to show. The
very smoothness and ease with which he manages them,
and the fervor of the passages in which they occur, are
likely to veil them from the twentieth-century reader who
associates puns with comedy and a coolly detached punster.

Herbert's most distinctive use of the figure enables him
to sustain two or more metaphorical systems throughout a
poem, to sound his imagerial notes in polyphonic fashion.
The phrase *poetic levels of meaning* has been much abused
in our time; among its many violations is the tendency
which some critics show to evoke it in description of pieces
containing families of imagery arranged in succession.
Much of Herbert's poetry, however, is genuinely multi-
levelled; and his feat of managing language so that several
metaphorical statements are offered at one time, and offered
without the fanfare of conspicuous ambiguity, makes his
verse very different from that of the other so-called metaphysical poets, whose practice it was to use different images
successively, not attendantly.

Donne, for one, even in the poems which depend most
fully on figurative language for the development of their
argument, and even in those which seem imagerially most
neatly organized, moves freely from one trope to another.

His method is not to sustain two figurative systems simultaneously, but rather to assemble a sequence of symbols all philosophically or even materially related. In *A Valediction: of Weeping,* for example, tears are associated with coins, then with wombs, then with newborn infants, then with globes which can be painted to signify the world, finally with tides which overflow the entire world. Each item of this symbolic repertory bears marked resemblance to the others: all are round (even the waters which cover the whole earth); all are instigated by the singer's beloved; all represent the transformation of a valueless object into something precious because of the reflected face of the lady. Donne has, then, selected and arranged his references with obvious care. Yet he does not ask us to think of tears as coins at the same time that we think of them as wombs or as worlds. These equivalents must be regarded as discrete. This method operates in most of his successful poems. In *A Valediction: Forbidding Mourning,* the physical separation of spiritually united lovers is likened to many things, most of them scientific phenomena—the dying of godly men, the almost imperceptible movement of the spheres, the ready malleability of gold, the sympathetic movement of the two feet of a compass—but the likenesses occur one at a time. Frequently Donne uses the same figure more than once within a poem, as he does the violet in *The Extasie,* but he does not intend the reader to keep it in mind between its appearances, in which interim he is rather led to contemplate twisted eye-beams, sweat-sealed hands, lovers as negotiating armies, lovers' bodies as sepulchral statues. A great part of Donne's proverbial ingenuity derives from his constant shifting from image to related image, not from maintaining several tissues of imagery one on top of the other.

In most of Herbert's poems, however, the imagery is laminar. In *Vanitie* (I), for example, he has evolved a complex metaphorical structure for showing the funda-

mental similarity of vain pursuits, even though each may
appear singular and fruitful to its unwise devotee. For
Herbert, the pleasures of the world were gifts of God to be
enjoyed, but they became vanities, not blessings, if they
distracted man from contemplation of their Maker. The
truly wise man, he felt, always sought not merely the satis-
faction of the things themselves, but God in the things of
the world. The first three stanzas of this poem recount
three searches for infra-Godly goods:

> The fleet Astronomer can bore,
> And thred the spheres with his quick-piercing minde:
> He views their stations, walks from doore to doore,
> Surveys, as if he had design'd
> To make a purchase there: he sees their dances,
> And knoweth long before
> Both their full-ey'd aspects, and secret glances.
>
> The nimble Diver with his side
> Cuts through the working waves, that he may fetch
> His dearely-earned pearl, which God did hide
> On purpose from the ventrous wretch:
> That he might save his life, and also hers,
> Who with excessive pride
> Her own destruction and his danger wears.
>
> The subtil Chymick can devest
> And strip the creature naked, till he finde
> The callow principles within their nest:
> There he imparts to them his minde,
> Admitted to their bed-chamber, before
> They appear trim and drest
> To ordinarie suitours at the doore. (85)

In a number of ways, the three men are quite various.
Each is interested in a different kind of unknown; each
explores a different physical element: the goal of the
astronomer is intellectual, that of the diver material (surely
his name is intended to remind us of his quest for riches),
that of the alchemist a mixture of the two. And yet the

three men are made to demonstrate an ineluctable sameness of method and purpose, both by the way that Herbert so carefully parallels their cases, and, more important, by the ambiguity of the language in which their work is described. All three are, in some measure, destroyers. Herbert takes the familiar metaphor of the astronomer's threading the spheres (originating, probably, in diagrams of the universe in which the lines tracing planetary orbits look much like strings transfixing the heavenly bodies) and renders it to convey an impression of damage: the astronomer *bores* and *pierces* the bodies with his mind, thereby reducing their magic and mystery. The diver *cuts through* the waves to achieve the *destruction* of the shellfish bearing the pearl. And the chemist, who doubtless conceives himself as seeking naked truth, is intensified into a bird of prey who *can divest and strip the creature naked* to discover its components. The common ultimate achievement of these men is death, because of their materialistic vision of God's creation.[2]

Each unwittingly shares a second characteristic with the others. His activity is a misdirected kind of love—on one level, the love of God's works more than of Him; on another, a debased kind of earthly love, or lust. Herbert uses some astronomical jargon (*stations, aspects, glances, full ey'd,* and *purchase,* which then meant concubinage as well as the application of mechanical force) both in its technical sense and also to suggest a man making a selection at a bordello, implying a person interested in planets but not in heaven to be analogous to the victim of fleshly lust. The diver comes close to raping the oyster for her pearl; while the alchemist, unlike ordinary lay suitors, gains the very bed-chamber of his experimental subject.

The point is that Herbert, unlike Donne, frequently maintains his important metaphors continuously and simultaneously. While the intellectual pleasure of reading one of the *Songs and Sonnets* consists of following the frequently

dazzling modulations of imagery, that afforded by the
poems in *The Temple* lies in one's apprehension of co-
existing figures. More often than not, this coexistence
provides the "point" of the verse. Certainly this is true in
Vanitie (I), where, in the concluding stanza, Herbert
points out that but one search, that for God, brings ful-
filling unity, love instead of lust, life instead of death:

> What hath not man sought out and found,
> But his deare God? who yet his glorious law
> Embosomes in us, mellowing the ground
> With showres and frosts, with love & aw,
> So that we need not say, Where's this command?
> Poore man, thou searchest round
> To finde out *death,* but missest *life* at hand.

The continuum of the overlapping lust and death imagery
of the first three stanzas, imagery introduced through
ambiguous words, gives full purpose to the love and life
statements of the last.

Similar overlays occur in *The Foil,* where Herbert calls
man to account for perversely refusing to regard the beauty
effected by virtue and the grief inevitably occasioned by sin:

> If we could see below
> The sphere of vertue, and each shining grace
> As plainly as that above doth show;
> This were the better skie, the brighter place.
>
> God hath made starres the foil
> To set off vertues; griefs to set off sinning:
> Yet in this wretched world we toil,
> As if grief were not foul, nor vertue winning. (175-76)

Through ambiguity of language he makes two simultaneous
metaphorical pronouncements. The dichotomy is visible,
if one would only allow himself to see it; and second, virtue
and sin are not only opposites, but warring quantities. One
meaning of *foil,* that of a thin sheet of metal commonly set

under jewels to enhance their brilliance, serves to indicate the clarity with which the stars make virtue shine and with which grief points out sin. God has, then, arranged for these two quantities to be manifestly plain, just as the facets of a gem appear most distinctly when it is mounted on foil. But *foil* also denotes a standard weapon, here, employed in a figurative engagement between virtue and sin. *Toil,* in Herbert's day, meant to fight as well as to labor, and thus worldly man is shown to ally himself in a skirmish which can have but one outcome, for, as we are assured in the last line, virtue is the inevitable winner, whereas sin is *foul*—both loathsome and a breaker of the rules of the contest. The two systems of configuration, those of fighting and the setting of jewels, conjoin to vivify Herbert's theme. Only man's perverse winking at the obvious nature of the antagonists prevents his understanding of this outcome.

Affliction (V) celebrates the Fortunate Fall, a theme ever attractive to Herbert, by comparing the placidity of Eden and the troubled, though eventually transcendent, course of the ark of Christ's church:

> My God, I read this day,
> That planted Paradise was not so firm,
> As was and is thy floting Ark; whose stay
> And anchor thou art onely, to confirm
> And strengthen it in ev'ry age,
> When waves do rise, and tempests rage.
>
> At first we liv'd in pleasure;
> Thine own delights thou didst to us impart:
> When we grew wanton, thou didst use displeasure
> To make us thine: yet that we might not part,
> As we at first did board with thee,
> Now thou wouldst taste our miserie.
>
> There is but joy and grief;
> If either will convert us, we are thine:
> Some Angels us'd the first; if our relief

Take up the second, then thy double line
  And sev'rall baits in either kinde
  Furnish thy table to thy minde.

  Affliction then is ours;
We are the trees, whom shaking fastens more,
While blustring windes destroy the wanton bowres,
And ruffle all their curious knots and store.
  My God, so temper joy and wo,
  That thy bright beams may tame thy bow. (97)

Several ambiguous words weigh the difference between the
garden and the ark and evaluate the effects of free will.
Planted, in the first stanza, refers both to the flora of the
initial habitation and to its absolute fixity, a limitation
removed from the floating ark, which enjoys both freedom
of motion and, paradoxically, the stability of the divine
anchor. This twofold implication is expanded in the final
strophe. *Board,* in the second stanza, designates the First
Parents' living with God and also Noah's entry of the ark;
baits, in the third, doubles to name the gustatory dainties
of Paradise and the lure of trouble employed on the ark.

 The ark itself, as Hutchinson points out, doubtless
symbolizes the church and its members, an association
which Herbert as a clergyman had brought to mind afresh
whenever he read the Baptismal Office. The close of the
first stanza, then, denotes both the firmness of the ark-
church and the more explicit mercy toward its individual
members mentioned in the Prayer for Absolution in the
Order for Holy Communion ("Confirm and strengthen you
in all goodness, and bring you to everlasting life: through
Jesus Christ our Lord"). The ark of the Old Testament
was, however, sometimes glossed as Christ Himself, the
Refuge of all in time of trouble.[3] Herbert was aware of this
interpretation, as is clear in *The Sacrifice*:

 My silence rather doth augment their crie;

> My dove doth back into my bosome flie,
> Because the raging waters still are high. . . . (29)

This secondary significance would give additional weight to the bow of the concluding stanza of *Affliction* (V). The bow of the covenant with Noah gives way not to an instrument of wrath, but to the tamed and tempered bow of Christ the Divine Cupid. The affliction of the fall, then, produces the love of Christ for the church.

In *The Family,* to my mind one of the most unfortunately neglected of Herbert's poems, the poet wishes for order of soul. He exemplifies this order by means of two figures: human faculties exercised in consort make music, whereas indecorously indulged they produce noise; and, as the title indicates, the faculties of the well-ordered man are a happy household, a fitting seat for the Lord to occupy. Perhaps because of the explanation inherent in the title, the musical imagery dominates the first stanza:

> What doth this noise of thoughts within my heart,
>   As if they had a part?
> What do these loud complaints and puling fears,
>   As if there were no rule or eares? (136)

Unruly thoughts make a *noise,* but each sounds as insistently as if it were taking a musical *part;* the noise is *loud* to the *eares,* since it follows no *rule.* Yet *rule* is also suggestive of the family imagery; *puling,* too, is significant both as a kind of noise and as the sound which the children of the family might make.

Herbert continues to establish Christ as the absent Lord of the house:

> But, Lord, the house and familie are thine,
>   Though some of them repine.
> Turn out these wranglers, which defile thy seat:
>   For where thou dwellest all is neat.

The two central stanzas characterize the seat with some specificity. First, they focus on the outer parts of the estate:

> First Peace and Silence all disputes controll,
> > Then Order plaies the soul;
> And giving all things their set forms and houres,
> > Makes of wilde woods sweet walks and bowres.

Plaies recalls the musical imagery, though it, like *puling,* countersuggests the young members of the family; *set forms* implies something about both the strictly disciplined music which is correlative for the harmonious soul, and the well organized family group. By the penultimate strophe, we are in the house itself:

> Joyes oft are there, and griefs as oft as joyes;
> > But griefs without a noise:
> Yet speak they louder then distemper'd fears.
> > What is so shrill as silent tears?

Here Herbert avoids the oversimplified allegory which, in stanzas three and four, he seems headed for. Even in the soul of utmost integrity, there will be grief: but in this soul, the grief will upset none of the harmony. Several words from the "noisy" first stanza are repeated to point up the contrast: the griefs, unlike the thoughts, are *without a noise,* yet their silence, unlike that of *distemper'd* (out of tune) or *puling fears* is eloquent. It is *shrill,* and in the selection of this word Herbert shows his great mastery of purveying the subtle idea by means of the simple word. For in his time, the word meant thrilling and poignant as well as piercing in sound. Puling and distempered fears make a sharp sound, but silent grief pipes ditties to the spirit, to make Herbert quote one of his later admirers.

Only with these members of a household in residence, the poem concludes, will the lord reside continuously in his seat:

This is thy house, with these it doth abound:
      And where these are not found,
Perhaps thou com'st sometimes, and for a day;
      But not to make a constant stay.

The chief metaphors of *Affliction* (IV) are drawn from the Old Testament, especially from the Psalms, and from the book of Job, the great Biblical storehouse of *logia* about the troubled human being. Herbert relies heavily on the figures of man as broken vessel and man persecuted by his enemies, in many cases echoing Job closely. Much of the artistry of Herbert's poem lies in his coordination of the imagery of battle and that of the broken vessel, and in repeating some of the very words and phrases with which his protagonist initially complains of his difficulties to point up his final resignation to God's will. Like Job, who, we are told, was more blessed at the end of his life than at its beginning, he comes to understand that the man who has survived afflictions emerges stronger than the one perpetually sheltered, and pronounces himself ready to be rebuilt by God's powers into a vessel worthy of heaven. But at first, the value of his affliction escapes him. He complains of being *broken in pieces all asunder, a wonder tortured in the space | betwixt this world and that of grace,* of his knife-like thoughts *wounding my heart | with scatter's smart, | As watring pots give flowers their lives,* of his powers being *at strife,* in a plot to *kill them and me.* The two metaphors of distress are united. As earthenware container, *he is broken in pieces, tortured* (as is the piece of clay on the potter's wheel), pierced like a watering pot. Yet *tortured* serves doubly with this figure and with that of the man preyed upon by his foes; and his thought *wound* his heart just as the knife cuts the holes in the watering pot. And overcome by grievance, he fails to perceive that there is some hope in his affliction. He is, after all, turned and pulled away from this world toward that of grace,

and it is the piercing of the watering pot that enables it to
vivify the plants with the scattering of water. By the end
of the poem, however, he has entrusted himself and his
capabilities to God, confident that with this guidance, they
will work for his immortality:

> . . . Dissolve the knot,
> As the sunne scatters by his light
> All the rebellions of the night.

Then shall those powers, which work for grief,
> Enter thy pay,
> And day by day,
Labour thy praise, and my relief;
> With care and courage building me,
> Till I reach heav'n, and much more, thee.   (90)

Scattering is now recognized as the wholesome action which
has previously remained hidden from the speaker; his
powers work not for strife but for God; and the torturing
becomes the method by which he will be rebuilt and fitted
for heaven. Affliction is not idle.

In many of his poems, then, Herbert designs syn-
chronous combinations of metaphor by selecting words
applicable to more than one figurative system. A list of
such poems could easily be extended beyond those just
analyzed. In *Deniall* the supplicant deals with both military
and musical instruments; in *Praise* (III), the spinning
wheel with which the speaker resolves to spin God's praise
overlaps with the wheels of business, those of Pharoah's
chariot, and those of a press; in *Confession,* the same words
characterize grief as both guest and artisan; in *The Search,*
Herbert's failure to find a harmonious relationship with
God is narrated in terms of the music which he cannot
sound, and the barriers separating him from heaven, with
certain words (*keyes* and *barres,* for example) linking the
two imageries; in *Longing,* he blends the language of sickness and starvation to characterize the symptoms of his

yearning. And it would be difficult to find a single strophe of *The Sacrifice* which does not manifest in a doubly-charged word or two the terrible discrepancy between Christ's nature and His scornful treatment.

These poems with two-storied figuration decorously trace the processes of meditation. One never muses on but one thing at a time, of course, and the knowledge that the "simplest" thought represents an intricate complex of assertion and qualification is not a discovery of modern psychology, as every reader of Renaissance poetry has long since perceived. The serious meditative poets of the time found various ways to suggest the interaction of ideas involved in the most commonplace statement. Southwell was able to do a great deal with oxymora and the ironic employment of romantic clichés to describe his love for Christ. Donne, needless to say, was able to do much more with a greater variety of devices, but he purveyed the convolutions of thought principally through images calculated to demonstrate the wide range of his experience and through the dramatic shifting of argument from stanza to stanza. Herbert, like Donne, had a large bag of techniques which he used to arrive at an accurate rendering of the cries of the heart, but certainly chief among them was his highly unusual custom of sustaining two or more families of metaphor throughout a poem and thereby giving multidimensional treatment to his theme. His devotional writing included many of the elements of his devotional thinking, and in similar combinations.

One of Herbert's remarkable gifts is that of preventing an effect of overingeniousness, despite the high concentration of his imagery. Going through *The Temple,* one never feels, as he is likely to do when he reads some of the immediate forerunners of the Augustans, that here is an extraordinarily witty bit of verse, nor is he mentally clogged at the end of a poem, as he frequently is when he has finished one of Lord Herbert's odes. Feeling balances thought in *The Temple,* even though thought is brilliantly recorded. Herbert obviously felt intensely, more so, probably, than his brother or Cleveland or Davenant. Yet he seems to have taken pains to minimize the intellectual effect of his complex imagery—an effort I will discuss more fully later. Let it suffice to remark here that while his language is always unassuming, it becomes more so in proportion to the density of the figuration. The words which serve to blend systems of imagery are regularly short and familiar—such as *planted, sun, glances, sit,* and *bow.* Delicacy of idea is conveyed in the easiest of phrases.

Herbert does not sustain concomitant systems of imagery in all of his poems: one of his excellences is his refusal to proliferate any single technique. Almost all of the verses in *The Temple,* however, contain puns which briefly introduce new metaphorical dimensions by overlapping two or more figures. A partial catalogue of them should demonstrate their prevalence and the instrumental role which they play in his work.

The Church-porch. The reader is warned of the folly of gambling:

> Play not for gain, but sport. Who playes for more
> Then he can lose with pleasure, stakes his heart;
> Perhaps his wives, too, and whom she hath bore:
> Servants and churches also play their part.
>   Onely a herauld, who that way doth passe,
>   Findes his crackt name at length in the
>   church-glasse. (14)

A.D. has pointed out that *cracked* was a seventeenth-century expression for bankrupt.[4] The crazing of the glass, then, symbolizes the brokenness of his life and name.

The Sacrifice. Christ comments on the indignities of His treatment: "Behold, they spit on me in scornfull wise, / Who by my spittle gave the blinde man eies." (31) In Herbert's time *spittle* was, of course, the common form of *hospital;* he himself used it (spelled the same way) in line 183 of *The Thanksgiving.* Here the word is employed in both senses to point up Christ's charitable healing and to contrast it with the rudeness of His tormentors.[5]

The Thanksgiving. Herbert questions the appropriateness of musical treatment of the Passion:

> Shall I then sing, skipping thy dolefull storie,
> And side with thy triumphant glorie?
> Shall thy strokes be my stroking? thorns, my flower? (35)

Strokes refers to the blows dealt Christ, but *stroking* is a multiple pun: the speaker muses on the irony of any part of the Passion having the power to soothe, or comfort, as Hutchinson has pointed out (p. 487). *Strokes* and *stroking* were also familiar musical terms at the time. The twenty-sixth of the *Outlandish Proverbs* reads "Great strokes make not sweete musick." Stroking, then, Herbert implies here, is doubly unsuitable as provoker of pleasure in general and as technique of music in particular.

Three lines below in the same poem, Herbert muses on the difficulty of rendering even an accurate account of the Crucifixion: "But how then shall I imitate thee, and / Copie thy fair, though bloudie hand?" *Hand* provides a witty yet painful bridge between the event of the Death and the poet's effort to imitate it in verse: in handwriting, Herbert will attempt to describe Christ's handwound.

The Agonie. Here is an obvious, but, as far as I know, unnoticed pun: "Sinne is that presse and *vice,* which forceth pain / To hunt his cruell food through ev'ry vein." (37)

Easter. With most tender humor, Herbert ambiguously describes the Resurrection in terms of everyday human action: "I got me flowers to straw thy way; / I got me boughs off many a tree: / But thou wast up by break of day. . . ." (42)

Repentance. Meditating on the brevity of life and the

need for God's grace during its short span, the poet exclaims:
"Oh! gently treat / With thy quick flow'r, thy momentarie
bloom. . . ." (48) The primary meaning of *quick* here is
alive or lifegiving; but the conjunction of *quick flow'r* and
momentarie bloom urges the reader also to consider the
meaning rapid, and so to contrast the quickness of God's
powers with the ephemeral flower of humanity.

Faith. Through two stanzas Herbert by means of
carefully selected language figures God as a theatrical
producer:

> When creatures had no reall light
> Inherent in them, thou didst make the sunne
> Impute a lustre, and allow them bright;
> And in this *shew,* what Christ hath done.
>
> That which before was darkned clean
> With bushie groves, pricking the *lookers* eie,
> Vanisht away, when Faith did *change the scene.* (51)[6]

The H. Communion. Herbert contemplates the miracle of the conjunction of heaven and earth occurring during
the sacrament. To him, the most marvelous aspect of the
union is Christ's condescension to grace the earthiest of all
earthly phenomena, His creature of dust. Two bivalent
uses of *earth* denote both the great and small worlds:

> Before that sinne turn'd flesh to stone,
>   And all our lump to leaven;
> A fervent sigh might well have blown
>   Our innocent earth to heaven.
>
> For sure when Adam did not know
>   To sinne, or sinne to smother;
> He might to heav'n from Paradise go,
>   As from one room t'another.
>
> Thou hast restor'd us to this ease
>   By this thy heav'nly bloud;
> Which I can go to, when I please [another pun]
>   And leave th' earth to their food. (53)

Love (II). The poem is infused with the imagery of sickness (Man is blinded by wit, which operates in the service of lust, but God will mend his eyes) and law. Both conjoin in one ambiguous word: "Thou shalt recover all thy goods in kinde, / Who wert *disseized* by usurping lust. . . ." (54)

In the course of another poem, *The Temper* (I), Herbert again plays upon a legal term, as the speaker gradually resigns himself to the difficulty of trying to extend himself between heaven and earth:

> O rack me not to such a vast extent;
>
> .   .   .   .   .
>
> Yet take thy way; for sure thy way is best;
>   Stretch or contract me, thy poore debter:
>   This is but tuning of my breast,
>   To make the musick better. (55)

Contract, as John Hollander has observed, belongs to two families of imagery: shorten me, the poet is saying, if as a result I can make better music; also put me under contract to You, since I am already Your debter.[7]

The H. Scriptures (I). Herbert describes the Bible as the book which reveals heaven to earth. Among the details of this description is the statement that "thou art heav'ns Lidger here." (58) *Lidger,* as Hutchinson comments (p. 496), is "one appointed to 'lie' or reside at a foreign court, a resident ambassador." But in a poem about a book, particularly one setting down records, surely the word must also be read as a pun on *ledger.*

The H. Scriptures (II). In the first of the pair, Herbert has characterized Holy Writ as a healer. The second contains complementary imagery:

> This verse marks that, and both do make a motion
>   Unto a third, that ten leaves off doth lie:
>   Then as dispersed herbs do watch a potion,
> These three make up some Christians destinie. . . . (58)

The pages of the Bible, digested in significant combination by the wise reader, yield a spiritual medicine far superior to the potion formed by the blending of plants. The ambiguity of *leaves* establishes the metaphor.

Mattens. Herbert offers the petition that with each sunrise man may review his awareness of the Creator in the creation. The poem concludes with a compound metaphor:

> Teach me thy love to know;
> That this new light, which now I see,
> May both the work and workman show:
> Then by a sunne-beam I will climbe to thee. (63)

God, the workman, has included beams among the materials of His building; on a beam of light, newly available each morning, man can climb the *scala meditatoria*.

Herbert, like Donne, sometimes designated God as the All of the universe (a notable example in Donne occurs in the second sonnet of *La Corona*). In *The Invitation*, Herbert concludes by saying that he has invited everyone to God's board: "For it seems but just and right / In my sight, / Where is All, there All should be." (180) In two of his poems, he seems to use *all* ambiguously, including the idea of God in the word. *The Quidditie* ends with his famous assessment of the value of poetry: "But it is that which while I use / I am with thee, and *most take all*." (70) A. D. has pointed out that *most take all* is a proverb, evidently a gambling term, meaning "to scoop the pool."[8] Herbert wins, then, when he writes poetry, since he feels himself in the presence of God. In this context, however, it strongly suggests the superimposed meaning of Herbert's *most* partaking of God through poetry. Similarly in *An Offering*, when he refers to the healing powers of Christ, he appears to invest the word with double meaning:

> There is a balsome, or indeed a bloud,
> Dropping from heav'n, which doth both cleanse and close

All sorts of wounds; of such strange force it is.
Seek out this All-heal. . . . (147)

It is a Godly cure-all.

Sunday. Falconry imagery, a favorite with Herbert, figures conspicuously in the last stanza:

> Thou art a day of mirth:
> And where the week-dayes trail on ground,
> Thy flight is higher, as thy birth.
> O let me take thee at the bound,
> Leaping with thee from sev'n to sev'n,
> Till that we both, being toss'd from earth,
> Flie hand in hand to heav'n! (76-77)

In the second stanza, however, this imagery overlaps with that of the week as a man, and consequently is frequently overlooked:

> The other dayes and thou
> Make up one man; whose face thou art,
> Knocking at heaven with thy brow:
> The worky-daies are the back-part;
> The burden of the week lies there,
> Making the whole to stoup and bow,
> Till thy release appear.

The heaviness of the week days causes the time-man to stoop over and bow down, to be brought upright only by the return of Sunday. But *stoup* and *release* are part of the argot of falconry. Here, as in the conclusion of the poem, Sunday promotes the attainment of height through *release*: the other days instigate a downward flight.

Sighs and Grones. Herbert confesses his unworthiness: ". . . My lust / Hath still sow'd fig-leaves to exclude thy light. . . ." He alludes, clearly, to the First Parents' sewing fig leaves together to make aprons when they discover their nakedness. But he puns on *sow'd*; the speaker of the poem is the steward of God, and here the pitch of his defection

is his planting this symbol of sensuality on his lord's land.
Herbert's spelling is singularly consistent for his time, as
Hutchinson has observed, and every time that the word
sow (and its grammatical variants) appears in *The Temple,*
it denotes planting ("Church Militant" 107, *Sion* 9, *The
Discharge* 15). In this passage, then, the sinner outdoes
Adam and Eve: they merely fasten the leaves together,
while he propagates them.

Lent. Herbert praises fasting in terms sufficiently
ambiguous to suggest the related virtue of chastity:

> Besides the cleannesse of sweet abstinence,
> Quick thoughts and motions at a small expense,
> > A face not fearing light:
> Whereas in fulnesse there are sluttish fumes,
> Sowre exhalations, and dishonest rheumes,
> > Revenging the delight. (86)

The Pearl. "I know the wayes of Learning; bothe the
head / And pipes that feed the presse, and make it runne.
. . ." (88) This enigmatic beginning has occasioned its
share of speculative comment. Oley proposed that the pipes
were "those Horns of Oyl, the two Universities"; Beeching
suggested, correctly I think, that Herbert refers to the
printing press; Hutchinson points out the probable reference to the allegorization in Zechariah 4:12-14 of the
golden candlestick: "And I answered again, and said unto
him, What be these two olive branches which through the
two golden pipes empty the golden oil out of themselves?
And he answered me and said, Knowest thou not what these
be? And I said, No, my Lord. Then said he, These are
the two anointed ones, that stand by the Lord of the whole
earth."[9] If Herbert had the prophet in mind, then *head*
would be a pun, at once naming Christ as the Head of the
anointed ones, and the head of the printing press. Yet it
would be incongruous, I feel, for the protagonist of the
poem to reject, or at least to judge insufficient, the kind of

learning disseminated by the Head through His apostles,
and the kinds of knowledge enumerated in the remainder
of the stanza are unequivocally secular. The Scriptures
were, Herbert made clear in the fourth chapter of *A Priest
to the Temple,* the chief and top of the parson's knowledge;
they should, moreover, be supplemented by a consultation
of the "Commenters and Fathers." I propose, rather, that
Herbert was thinking of the printing press (a popularizer
of learning) and of the two channels of knowledge mentioned by Sir John Davies in the *Hearing* section of *Nosce
Teipsum*:

> Thus by the organs of the Eye and Ear
> The Soul with knowledge doth herself endue:
> 'Thus she her prison may with pleasure bear,
> Having such prospects, all the world to view.'

> These conduit-pipes of knowledge feed the Mind,
> But the other three attend the Body still.[10]

Here is the kind of general knowledge which Herbert
judges insufficient in itself; the *head* of *The Pearl,* if this
association is correct, is both the head of the press and the
head of the human being, where the two nobler senses are
located. That Herbert was in accord with most Renaissance
men in regarding sight and hearing as the two senses
serving knowledge is evident from "The Church-porch,"
where one is enjoined to divert his mind from other people
in church and to attend to the preacher:

> In time of service seal up both thine eies,
>
> .   .   .   .   .
>
> These doores being shut, all by the eare comes in.   (23)

Herbert's recollection of this section of *Nosce Teipsum*
is further attested by the emphasis which Davies places on
the ear as a labyrinth. Each ear, he says, is a complex of
"mazes"; "with turns and winding oft" it delays sound so

that it does not pierce the brain too violently; in its
"labyrinth" it stays the voice.[11] This reading, which pre-
serves the ambiguity that Hutchinson senses in the passage,
seems to me preferable in light of the rest of the poem.

   Jordan (II). The first two stanzas abound in words of
double purport:

> When first my lines of heav'nly joyes made mention,
> Such was their lustre, they did so excell,
> That I sought out quaint words, and trim invention;
> My thoughts began to burnish, sprout, and swell,
> Curling with metaphors a plain intention,
> Decking the sense, as if it were to sell.
>
>   .   .   .   .   .
>
> I often blotted what I had begunne;
> This was not quick enough, and that was dead.
> Nothing could seem too rich to clothe the
>   sunne. . . . (102)

Burnish, as Hutchinson points out (p. 513), means to spread
out as well as to polish, and so complements both *lustre*
and *sprout and swell; sense* surely refers at once to the
matter of *invention* and to the sensuous appeal of his verse;
quick (see Hutchinson again) means both rapid and alive;
and *sunne* contains the double reference so frequently
found in *The Temple,* given sanction in the poem of that
name.

   Obedience. Here, as several commentators have observed, Herbert uses the language of law to describe spiritual rededication. With the giving of this poem to God,
he legally conveys himself and all that he has to the Buyer.
Several of the important words are puns. In the second
stanza, *Deed* surely carries the significance of an action as
well as a legal document: "To which I do agree, / And here
present it as my speciall Deed." (104) Two stanzas later,
he contemplates the many goods bequeathed to him by
God: "O let thy sacred will / All thy delight in me fulfill!"

Will patently refers to a figurative legal document in which the goods are assigned, as well as the broader meaning of God's wishes concerning man. Herbert moves to the Passion:

> Besides, thy death and bloud
> Showed a strange love to all our good:
> Thy sorrows were in earnest; no faint proffer,
> Or superficiall offer
> Of what we might not take, or be withstood.

Earnest works much the same way as *will;* Christ's sorrows were both sincere, and, in the legal context, the earnest money by which He marked the good faith of His bargain for mankind.

   Sion. Herbert contrasts the ceremony by means of which God was served in Solomon's temple with the simplicity of worship under the Covenant of Grace. Most of the details of temple worship incorporated in the poem are architectural (as is true also of the account in I Kings); yet the ambiguity of a few of them suggests musical praise:

> Lord, with what glorie wast thou serv'd of old,
> When Solomons temple stood and flourished!
>   Where most things were of purest gold;
>   The wood was all embellished.
>
>   .   .   .   .   .
>
> Yet all this glorie, all this pomp and state
> Did not affect thee much, was not thy aim. . . . (106)

Flourished, embellished, and *pomp* are musical terms. *A flourish* was a fanfare; an *embellishment,* what the modern musician would call a *mordant* or a *turn;* and a *pomp,* the kind of music played at a ceremonious procession. These suggestions of elaborate and ornate music are complemented by the simple and infinitely less impressive praise of the contrite heart:

All Solomons sea of brasse and world of stone
Is not so deare to thee as one good grone.

And truly brasse and stones are heavie things,
Tombes for the dead, not temples fit for thee:
   But grones are quick, and full of wings,
   And all their motions upward be;
And ever as they mount, like larks they sing:
The note is sad, yet musick for a King.[12]

Dialogue. Herbert has the speaker question God's concern with so poor a creature as himself:

    Sweetest Saviour, if my soul
      Were but worth the having,
    Quickly should I then controll
      Any thought of waving. (114)

God assures him that the concern is His business, where-upon the protagonist argues further:

    But as I can see no merit,
      Leading to this favour:
    So the way to fit me for it
      Is beyond my savour.

Hutchinson glosses *waving,* explaining that *wave* is an old variant spelling of *waive.* It is, then, a pun with legal associations, meaning both to hesitate and to give up the right to. *Savour,* also, is a pun. Here Herbert uses it to mean both good taste, complementing the *Sweetest Saviour* of the first stanza, and to mean understanding. In his near-despair, then, the speaker disclaims both desire for and comprehension of the favor of God. The word works comparably in *An Offering*: "Yet thy favour / May give savour / To this poore oblation. . . ." (148)

Love Unknown. Three kinds of purification of the corrupt heart are explained—remedies for the heart which is foul, hard, and dull. In the central section an ambiguous verb points up the error by which the speaker's heart has become hard:

> So I went
> To fetch a sacrifice out of my fold,
> Thinking with that, which I did thus present,
> To warm his love, which I did fear grew cold.
> But as my heart did tender it, the man,
> Who was to take it from me, slipt his hand,
> And threw my heart into the scalding pan;
> My heart, that brought it (do you understand?)
> The offerers heart. *Your heart was hard, I fear.* (129-30)

A burnt-offering sacrifice is not adequate: one's oblation must come from within, or his heart will be stony. In the fifth line quoted above, the worshipper attempts to *tender* or offer a material appeasement; he is straightway shown that a softened or *tender* heart is the only acceptable sacrifice.

Divinitie. Herbert takes to task those who attempt to complicate Christ's lucid revelations:

> Could not that Wisdome, which first broacht the wine,
>   Have thicken'd it with definitions?
> And jagg'd his seamlesse coat, had that been fine,
>   With curious questions and divisions? (134)

In the context of a passage dealing with conversation, and with the undue multiplication of intellectual exercise, *broacht* clearly means to introduce as a subject of discussion; also, of course, it signals the opening of the winecask, and so prepares the way for the second cutting action, the jagging of the seamless coat. Grosart pointed out another pun in the stanza, that on *fine.* Wouldn't it have been a fine thing, Herbert asks ironically, if the Creator had marred the integrity of Christ's simple robe with unnecessary ornament? But *fine* also means a fashionably cut garment, and thus suggests the worldliness which prompts

sophistical divines to wish for an unduly elaborate the-
ology.[13]

Grieve not the Holy Spirit. Herbert observes that a
musician, a man, can show greater contrition than inanimate objects of nature, no matter how penitent they may
appear to be:

> O take thy lute, and tune it to a strain,
>
> .   .   .   .   .
>
>   Marbles can weep; and surely strings
>   More bowels have, then such hard things.   (136)

He assumes two associations on the part of the reader: that
strings are made of cat gut, and that in the Pauline Epistles,
the bowels are consistently referred to as the seat of pity
and compassion. The gut strings of the lute, then, can be
made by the compassionate lutanist to evince more grief
than the weeping stone.

The Pilgrimage.

> That led me to the wilde of Passion, which
>   Some call the wold;
>   A wasted place, but sometimes rich,
>   Here I was robb'd of all my gold,
> Save one good Angell, which a friend had ti'd
>   Close to my side.   (142)

Grosart recognized the obvious pun implicit in *Angell;* and
Empson sees one with *willed-wilde, would-wold.* Empson
feels, further, that *Passion* should be considered in its
liturgical sense as well as an exercise of the sensual.[14]

The Jews. Herbert comments regretfully on the spiritual poverty which the Hebrew people have suffered since
their rejection of Christ: "Who by not keeping [their life-
stream] once, became a debter; / And now by keeping lose
the letter. . . ." (152) A. D. has observed that *letter* is a
pun; these lines, he feels, state that the Jews through Adam

failed to keep the law once, thereby becoming debters or sinners and placing themselves under the restraint of the Mosaic law; and now, by rejecting Christ but keeping the Mosaic law imperfectly, have lost access to the One Who lets Christians loose from both the sin of Adam and the strictures of Mosaic law.[15] *Letter,* then, denotes both the jots and tittles of the law and Christ as release from that law.

The same pun occurs in *Sepulchre,* a meditation on the miracle of Christ's releasing man from the hardness and coldness of the law, symbolized by the tomb, and coming to dwell in the heart. He is the letter, or releaser, of humanity:

> And as of old the Law by heav'nly art
> Was writ in stone; so thou, which also art
> The letter of the word, find'st no fit heart
> To hold thee. (41)

Grief. The poet asks all of the watery things of nature to supplement his tears. Finally, he turns to his verse in the hope that it, too, will aid his weeping: "Cease, be dumbe and mute, / Give up your feet and running to mine eyes. . . ." (164) *Running,* of course, doubles as the movement of the rhythm and the flowing of his tears.

The Glimpse. In a lament that delight should be so short-lived, Herbert puns, using the still-current expression for observing musical rhythm: "Me thinks delight should have / More skill in musick, and keep better time." (154)

The Forerunners. The poem opens with a mention of the white hairs which the speaker has found in his head, then continues with his meditation of these harbingers of death.

> But must they have my brain? must they dispark
> Those sparkling notions, which therein were bred?
> Must dulnesse turn me to a clod? (176)

As Hutchinson observes, *dispark* is a shortened form of
disempark, meaning to turn out of a park; Herbert is
thinking, then, of losing the thoughts which were bred in
his brain. Yet because of its contiguity to *sparkling,* it
becomes a pun meaning to take the sparkle away from his
ideas, to dull them. The same pun appears in *The Church
Militant*:

> Which [Pleasure] soon was blown to such a mightie
>   flame,
> That though our Saviour did destroy the fame,
> Disparking oracles, and all their treasure,
> Setting affliction to encounter pleasure.

The Rose. Don Cameron Allen has noted that the
poem begins with a pun inaugurating an ambiguity which
prevails for several stanzas:

> Presse me not to take more pleasure
>   In this world of sugred lies,
> And to use a larger measure
>   Then my strict, yet welcome size. (177)

The double reading demanded by *Presse* involves two
speakers: the rose begs not to be squeezed to yield its
perfumed essence (a process referred to later in the poem);
and at the same time a human speaker disclaims willing-
ness to become over-involved with the transient delights of
the world.[16]

The Invitation. Grosart glossed the triple meaning of
define in the second stanza: "Come ye hither All, whom
wine / Doth define. . . ." (180) "Define" him by his then
qualities, but also that his fineness or propriety peculiar to
man is taken (de) away or from him—a sub-play also on
"finis."[17]

Dooms-day. Herbert looks forward to the trumpet call
which will release the buried dead:

> Lord, thy broken consort raise,
> And the musick shall be praise. (187)

Consort denotes both the music which will be sounded here
and there, and to the damaged and schism-rent church, the
spouse of Christ.[18]

Euen-song (the discarded poem of the Williams MS.,
not the one of the same name in *The Temple*). Herbert
puns on *shade*:

> If thou deferr this light, then shadow mee:
> Least that the Night, earths gloomy shade,
> ffouling her nest, my earth invade,
>   As if shades knew not Thee. (203)

Punning, it should be said, was not a peculiarity of
Herbert's mature style, but he uses the device to infinitely
greater advantage in *The Temple* than in his early poems.
A few of the *double entendres* of the youthful poet are
almost smirkingly witty, though they avoid the offensiveness
of many contemporary ones; a great many of them, however, are not only acceptable but even praiseworthy. Even
as early as 1620 (the date assigned by Hutchinson to the
Musae Responsoraie, Herbert's earliest body of verse), one
finds him using the pun not solely to heighten momentarily,
but to fuse together in the multiple meanings of a single
word the important elements of a poem. In *De Super-
pelliceo* (XIV), for example, Herbert answers Melville's
denunciation in his *Anti-tami-cami-categoria* that the Anglican clergy, in wearing surplices, are trying to emulate
Christ. White, Herbert argues, is a holy color, one sanc-
tioned by Christ for the use of His creatures. He concludes
with a pun on *alb-alba-Albion* which succeeds admirably,
I feel, in superimposing the three "goods" championed:

> Ergo ringantur pietatis hostes,
> Filij noctis, populus malignus,

Dum suum nomen tenet, & triumphat
Albion albo. (390)

Trans. Therefore the enemies of piety are vexed, sons of
night, an evil people; meanwhile her name endures,
and Albion triumphs in the alb.

Equally apt are the puns at the end of *De Textore
Catharo* (XIX)—so appropriate for an Anglican apologist
to use in scoffing at a Psalm-singing weaver that had this
work been published earlier, doubtless they would have
become staple Royalist ammunition: the weaver *stamine,*
with stamina and with a warp [!] thread, twists Holy Writ
in the belief that he is an authority on both its text and the
texture of his product: "Et nunc perlongas Scripturae
stamine telas / Torquet, & in Textu Doctor vtroque cluet."
(392) (*Trans.* And now with thread he twists the long
webs of scripture, and is called a Doctor of both text and
texture.) Only slightly less good is the implied play on the
name of the angel coin in *In Simonem Magus,* the fourth
poem in *Lucus,* which Hutchinson estimates to have been
composed about 1623:

Nempe gravi fertur scelerata pecunia motu,
Si sursum iacias, in caput ipsa ruit.
Vnicus est nummus, caelo Christóque petitus,
Nempe in quo clarè lucet Imago Dei. (410)*

Trans. Tainted money is driven downward by its own
weight; if you throw it upward, it falls on its head.
There is only one coin, strived for by heaven and
Christ, in which shines brightly the image of God.

Or the one in *In Thomas Didymum,* where the pun on
proof-index finger underscores the extreme literal-minded-
ness of the doubter: "Et hoc indicium subis, Redemptor?"
(417) (*Trans.* And did you submit to this proof, Re-
deemer?)

During the eighteenth and nineteenth centuries, the

reputation of the pun suffered a series of massive wounds, emerging largely as part of the despised equipment of the false wit or of the composer of doggerel. Herbert's readers, consequently, closed their eyes to the fecundity of his doubly-charged expressions and thereby ignored much of his wit and thought him a singer of bland piety. Palmer, in the introduction which for decades modified students' critical apprehension of *The Temple,* found the poems admirable, among other reasons, because he felt Herbert to be free of the vicious punning characteristic of his age:

At a time when poets prided themselves on puns, he used few, and none of them jocosely. Verbal relationships arouse his curiosity, but never stir his mirth. The following is, I believe, a complete list: *dispark* and *sparkling* in *The Forerunners; do thee right* (write) in *Providence; heaven* and *haven* in *The Size; holy* and *wholly* in *Heaven; I ease you* in *Jesu; raise* and *raze* in *The Temper* and *The Sacrifice; rest* and *restlessness* in *The Pulley; strokes* and *stroking* in *The Thanksgiving; sonne* and *sunne* several times repeated and once discussed at length. Until within the last two hundred years, few writers of our language have abused it so little.[19]

Today few readers would wholly agree with Palmer and judge the pun an abomination, although the man is rare indeed who does not routinely groan at the punning of his fellows. But in the hands of an accomplished Renaissance poet the pun commands our respect, even as it was respected in the sixteenth and seventeenth centuries. Our widening knowledge of Renaissance phonology, for one thing, has enabled us to rediscover whole galaxies of multiple word meanings in the most elevated and sober poetry, involving what the eighteenth-century critic would have approved as true wit. A similarly increased awareness is the happy result of our century's investigation of Renaissance semantics; now that we know considerably more than our grandfathers about the meanings of Shakespeare's and Milton's and Sidney's words, and now that we know of their analogues in non-literary writing of the time, we are better equipped than our forebears to recognize dignified ambiguities and to take them seriously—to see them as anything but stylistic crudities.

Renaissance poets and theorists alike took them very seriously, so much so that they regarded them as much nearer the provenance of literary art than mere stylistic ornament. Aristotle had discussed them as one of the topics of invention, closely allied with the very logic of an argument: "The means by which we shall obtain an abundance of reasonings are four in number: (1) the provision of propositions, (2) the ability to distinguish in how many senses a particular expression is used, (3) the discovery of differences and (4) the investigation of similarities. The last three of these are also in a sense propositions; for it is possible to make a proposition in accordance with each of them."

It is with such high purpose, I believe, that Herbert customarily used the pun. For in *The Temple* it is seldom a trifling witty embellishment, added as an afterthought to the central argument of the poem. Rather, it serves as the most compact conceivable means of pointing up the sense of analogy, or, as frequently, of painful discrepancy between what is and what should be, which is the genesis of most of Herbert's meditations: one word is made the nexus of two imagerial systems. *Planted* in *Affliction* (V) knots the imagery of growth and vegetation with that of firmness and stability—the dual results of affliction, and the chief concerns of the poem; the bow in *Deniall* unites its military and musical motifs; the various sounds of *The Familie* simultaneously work with the musical figures and describe what one hears in the household of the soul. Here, as in a multitude of other poems in *The Temple,* the very structure and "idea" is embodied in the words with double meaning. In *The Sonne,* Herbert exclaims over the *neat-ness* of giving only one name to parents' issue and to the light of the heavens, and for Herbert, neatness was descriptive of the most scrupulous order and harmony, even the perfect balance of the universe. For him the neatness of the pun made possible the balance and harmony of some of his best poems.

3

Quiddities: The Titles

No poet writing in our language has made better or more original use of his titles than did George Herbert. The nicety that led Herbert to devise a celebrated variety of stanza forms for the expression of a remarkable range of religious emotions and ideas also led him to give his poems names that have numerous kinds of significance. Many of these have attracted the attention which they deserve. That some of them introduce a metaphorical dimension merely implied in the body of the poem, most readers are aware. *The Collar,* for example, does not contain overt reference to that item; *Church-lock and key* only indirectly equates sin with the key which closes God's ears; *The Quidditie* supports, but does not rename, its title; the same is true of *The Quip; Home* is about heaven, but heaven is called so only in the title; only in the title of *The Bunch of Grapes* is one directly reminded of the exploit of Joshua and Caleb; the title of *Giddinesse* is the sole one-word diagnosis of the inconstancy of man with which the poem deals; *Clasping of hands* depends upon its intertwining rhyme patterns, not metaphor, for the elucidation of the significance of this phrase; only in the title of *Josephs Coat* is the reader led to think specifically of the Old Testament story; the title of *The Pearl* clearly indicates Herbert's estimate of the value of the kingdom of heaven, yet the poem makes no extended use of the parable; "The Church-porch," an assortment of suggestions for the improvement of one's ethical nature, says clearly only in its heading that such improvement is necessary before one enters the church for refinement of the spirit. What caption could be more intellectually teasing than *Jordan*? or more purposely shocking than *The Bag,* in which Christ's sidewound is typified as a mailpouch in which messages may be sent to heaven? Who, besides Herbert, would invent names like *The Foil* and *The Forerunners*?

Some of Herbert's titles, however, do not enjoy the widespread appreciation which these do. Only fairly recently did Miss Tuve comment upon the heading of *The Temper* (I), which she rightly sees as a pun indicating both the tempering of the steel of the musical instrument alluded to, and also the restraint of the human spirit.[1] She has also pointed out the ambiguity of *Divinitie,* to which she correctly assigns a double allusion to knowledge of God and to the speculations of diviners, both of which figure prominently in the poem.[2] She has been of further help with the title of *A Parodie,* which, she shows, implies no element of burlesque of the secular lyric of which it is a variation; rather Herbert uses *parody* in the musical sense of the word, that is, to indicate that the poem sets new words to a well-known tune.[3]

The title of *Vertue* is a pun. Primarily, of course, it denotes just what we associate with the modern word *virtue*—goodness. Yet in the seventeenth century, it also conveyed the idea of strength or efficacy, a meaning surviving in our own day principally in the phrase *by virtue*

of. Surely both meanings are intended in this poem by
Herbert, for the conventionally beautiful things enumerated in the first three stanzas—daylight, roses, and spring—
have no power to resist even daily and seasonal ravages of
time, much less the destruction of the world. They are
sweet but weak or virtueless. The virtuous soul, however,
is strong, like seasoned timber:

> Onely a sweet and vertuous soul,
> Like season'd timber, never gives;
> But though the whole world turn to coal,
>   Then chiefly lives. (88)

Goodness, then, affords a power which the things of the
natural world cannot emulate.[4]

The title of *The Size* is also a pun. In addition to
carrying the meaning most familiar to modern readers,
that of magnitude, in Herbert's time it was also in common
usage as a shortened form of *assize,* also of an ordinance
or regulation, also, especially in Cambridge use, of an
allowance. All of these meanings are developed in the
imagery of the poem, though the legal ones predominate,
and all are fused into a coherent statement: God has
ordained that man should have only moderate joys in this
world, so that he can stand guiltless at the great judgment
and inherit the boundless joys of heaven.

> Content thee, greedie heart.
> Modest and moderate joyes to those, that have
> Title to more hereafter when they part,
>   Are passing brave.
>   .   .   .   .   .
>
> If thou hast wherewithall to spice a draught,
>   When griefs prevail;
>   And for the future time art heir
>   To th' Isle of spices, is't not fair?
>
>   To be in both worlds full
> Is more then God was, who was hungrie here.

Wouldst thou his laws of fasting disanull?

.   .   .   .   .

Thy Saviour sentenc'd joy,
And in the flesh condemn'd it as unfit,
At least in lump; for such doth oft destroy;
Whereas a bit
Doth tice us on to hopes of more,
And for the present health restore. (137-38)

The title, then, in one word combines the ideas of *moderation* as the *allowance* given by God so that man can be ready for the *judgment*.

A similar double statement is implied by the title of *The Crosse,* in which, after five stanzas of questioning the reason for being so physically delicate that he is unable fully to carry out his priestly duties, Herbert concludes on a note of resignation to being thwarted in his aspirations:

Ah my deare Father, ease my smart!
These contrarieties crush me: these crosse actions
Do winde a rope about, and cut my heart:
And yet since these thy contradictions
Are properly a crosse felt by thy Sonne,
With but foure words, my words, *Thy will be done.* (165)

The fact of his failure, of his being crossed in his wishes, proves his closest approximation to the agony of Christ on the cross.

Constancie details the qualities of the honest man. They are those of one who does not err, and throughout the poem Herbert enlists images of a straight-line journey to dramatize his fixity of purpose.

Who is the honest man?
He that doth still and strongly good pursue. . . .

.   .   .   .   .

Whose honestie is not
So loose or easie, that a ruffling winde
Can blow away, or glittering look it blinde:

Who rides his sure and even trot,
While the world now rides by, now lags behind.

   .   .   .   .   .

His goodnesse sets not, but in dark can runne. . . .

   .   .   .   .   .

Whom nothing can procure
When the wide world runnes bias from his will,
To writhe his limbes, and share, not mend the ill. (72-73)

The title, then, points more strongly to the functioning of this metaphor, to the progress of the pilgrim who does not wander or err, than to the non-metaphorical statements which Herbert makes about honesty.

The Reprisall follows *The Thanksgiving,* in which Herbert expresses gratitude for the Passion. Two kinds of tropes dominate the earlier poem. One is military:

O King of wounds . . .
Surely I will revenge me on thy love,
   And trie who shall victorious prove.

   .   .   .   .   .

The world and I will quarrel . . .
   O my deare Saviour, Victorie! (35-36)

The other is musical:

Shall I then sing, skipping thy doleful storie,
   And side with thy triumphant glorie?

   .   .   .   .   .

My musick shall finde thee, and ev'ry string
   Shall have his attribute to sing;
That all together may accord in thee,
   And prove one God, one harmonie.

In *The Reprisall,* Herbert concludes that the only worthy kind of thanksgiving for the Passion is confession. The title links it firmly with both systems of imagery contained in its predecessor. The most familiar sense of *reprisal,* of

course, is the military one—that of retaliation in warfare.
Atonement, then, is the retaliation most pleasing to Christ.
But *reprisal* is also a musical term meaning a return to the
original theme or subject, and thus this implication both
reminds us of the theme of *The Thanksgiving* and lends
poignance to the poet's plea for a return to innocence
through confession:

> O make me innocent, that I
> May give a disentangled state and free:
> And yet thy wounds still my attempts defie,
>   For by thy death I die for thee. (36)

The title of *Unkindnesse* carries the double significance
which the word commonly did in Herbert's time; it means
both lacking in compassion and unnatural. The refrain
of the lyric, which denounces the speaker's unwarrantably
bad treatment of God and emphasizes his neglect of his
reasonable duty as well as his callousness, is *I would not
use a friend as I use Thee;* this refrain is heightened to
Yet use I not my foes, as I use Thee in the last stanza. Both
Renaissance senses of *unkindness,* then, are intended in the
poem.

In *Content* Herbert explains that the happy man is the
one who discovers the riches within himself, the one who
need not wander in search of material pleasure. Thus the
two meanings of the title are inherent in the theme, meanings which the twentieth-century reader is likely to call
contentment and *contents.* Contentment is to be found in
the contents of one's own bosom:

> Peace mutt'ring thoughts, and do not grudge to keep
>   Within the walls of your own breast:
> Who cannot on his own bed sweetly sleep,
>   Can on anothers hardly rest.
>
> Gad not abroad at ev'ry quest and call
>   Of an untrained hope or passion.

.   .   .   .   .

Mark how the fire in flints doth quiet lie,
          Content and warm t' it self alone:
But when it would appeare to others eye,
          Without a knock it never shone.

.   .   .   .   .

Then cease discoursing soul, till thine own ground,
          Do not thy self or friends importune.
He that by seeking hath himself once found,
          Hath ever found a happie fortune. (68-69)

The title of *Redemption* refers primarily to Christ's action on behalf of mankind, as the word invariably must in any religious context, yet it also serves to call attention to the terms of the legalistic parable which Herbert has devised to refresh the reader's meditation on the Passion:

Having been tenant long to a rich Lord,
     Not thriving, I resolved to be bold,
     And make a suit unto him, to afford
A new small-rented lease, and cancell th' old. (40)

The tenant looks all over heaven and the rich places of the earth for his master, finally finding him among thieves and murderers: "There I him espied, / Who straight, *Your suit is granted,* said, & died." By insisting on the connection of *redemption* with human law, a connection usually forgotten in theological uses of the word, Herbert has drawn emphatic contrast between the Lord of his poem and the landlords of the world.

The general significance of the name of *The Pulley* is perfectly clear: man's weariness is the rope whereby God can toss man to His breast. The facetiousness of the title's tone, however, may have escaped some readers. Herbert might have taken it from a passage in Thomas Nashe's *The Prayse of the Red Herring,* where last resorts to salvation are discussed lightly indeed: "Let any Persian oppunge this, and, in spite of his hairie tuft or loue-locke he leaves

on the top of his crowne, to be pulld vp or pullied vp to
heauen by, Ile set my foot to his, & fight it out with him,
that their fopperly god is not so good as a red Herring."[5]
With an affectionate teasing possible only to one on most
intimate terms with God, Herbert postulates Him (who
has given man all of the possible gifts of the universe)
having to haul his creatures up to heaven by keeping them
tired and restless. Ostensibly God is gently mocked;
actually, the man who would have to be pulley'd to heaven
because of weariness is strongly so.

The obvious violence of *The Collar* has attracted more
twentieth-century readers than have the more tranquil
measures of other poems in *The Temple*. Its popularity,
however, undoubtedly due to the fact that here Herbert
sounds a good deal like Donne, has not induced universal
accord as to its meaning. It is a difficult poem, and the title
is not the least of its difficulties. Hutchinson comments
that "the collar was in common use to express discipline,
and 'to slip the collar' was often used figuratively.
Preachers would use the word *collar* of the restraint imposed by
conscience; for example, Daniel Dyke (ob. 1614) says that
religion 'will not teach thy servant to slip his neck out of
the collar, and to deny thee service and subjection.'"   (531)
Biblical sanction for this kind of restraint is, of course,
plentiful. Everyone knows Christ's injunction to "Take
my yoke upon you, and learn of me . . . for my yoke is easy,
and my burden is light," and undoubtedly the title is
designed to suggest this obedience as the duty of every
Christian, and so for the outburst of the speaker to be
in some measure the voice of everyman. Is there, however,
a more specific application of the word *collar*? Does Herbert
refer to the general disciplinary obligations of all godly
men, or might he be dramatizing a more personal objection
to the restraints of his own priesthood? Does the Collar, in
short, stand for the clerical collar as symbol of sacerdotal
austerity? It might, for while Anglican clergymen of

Herbert's time did not wear the kind of clerical collars that they now do, they had a specified garb different from that of the layman: "The ordinary costume of the Episcopalian clergy of the seventeenth-century was fixed at the opening of James the First's reign by the 74th canon, which enjoins 'That the archbishops and bishops shall not intermit to use the accustomed apparel of their degrees. Likewise all deans, masters of colleges, archdeacons, and prebendaries, in cathedral and collegiate churches (being priests or deacons), doctors in divinity, law, and physic, bachelors in divinity, masters of arts, and bachelors of law, having any ecclesiastical living, shall usually wear gowns with standing collars and sleeves strait at the hands.' "[6] Divines were to wear special collars, then. Perhaps the fractiousness dramatized in this poem is that of the clergyman irked by the disciplines of his office. Other evidence points to this possibility. *The Collar* does not appear in the Williams MS. and so was most probably written after Herbert took orders, and while the *I* of the poem is not necessarily Herbert himself, he would surely have been particularly sensitive to the restive stirrings of the clergy. And in the initial lines, he strikes *the board. Board,* of course, was synonymous with *table.* When Herbert used it, however, he usually meant the communion table, where one feasted on the elements of the Holy Communion.[7] There is, then, a strong likelihood that the protagonist sacrilegiously strikes the altar, an action improbable for a layman to perform. Quite possibly the title of *The Collar* signals the restraints of priesthood as well as those of the universally imposed yoke of God.

But surely it signals other quantities, too. A number of years ago Dan S. Norton and T. O. Mabbott suggested a *collar-choler* pun.[8] Undoubtedly they were right, for the poem is nothing if not a dramatization of a choleric man's rebellion, one who raves and grows more fierce and wild before submitting to the address of God. And G. P. V.

Akrigg has argued for yet another denotation of the title: he suggests that it means *The Caller,* pointing to the voice at the end which the speaker hears calling.[9] This suggestion is not as bizarre as it might sound. Herbert's poem shows many similarities to Donne's *To Mr. Tilman after He Had Taken Orders,* a piece in which he demonstrated by a close paraphrase of one of its lines his knowledge of "The Church-porch." Donne questions the ease of the transition from lay to clerical life in terms reminiscent of the imagery of *The Collar*:

> Thou whose diviner soule hath caus'd thee now
> To put thy hand unto the holy Plough . . .
> What bringst thou home with thee? how is thy mind
> Affected since the vintage? Dost thou finde
> New thoughts and stirrings in thee?

Most suggestively, he designs Tilman's vocation as his *Calling,* reminding him that he must combine knowledge of both the world of natural man and the graces of heaven: "Both these in thee, are in thy Calling knit, / And make thee now a blest Hermaphrodite."

It seems entirely possible that in the single word *collar* Herbert alluded to several of the motifs of this complex poem: the yoke of God which all must bear, the particular yoke of the clergyman, the choler demonstrated by the human speaker, and the divine Speaker of the conclusion. Only a Herbert could combine these most disparate meanings without grotesquery.

I do not wish to leave the impression that all titles in *The Temple* are this ingenious, or that Herbert's effort was to be ever captious in naming his poems. On the contrary, many are as conspicuously simple and unequivocal as, say, *The Collar* and *Jordan* are provocative. The designations *The Thanksgiving, Prayer, Love, The Sinner, Hope, Lovejoy,* and *Dulnesse*—to mention only a few—could scarcely indicate topics more central to the devotional concern of Herbert's seventeenth-century readers, and one could scarcely find words more typical of any religious vocabulary. Indeed, the felicity of many a title in his volume lies in the contrast between the generality of the subject which it introduces and the specificity of the experience set forth in the poem. *Sepulchre,* for example, postulates the true resting place of the Lord as the human heart; *The H. Communion* analyzes the architecture of the soul; *Conscience,* contrary to expectation, denegates the wholesomeness of that faculty (it is a prattler, an instigator of disease); *Paradise* is a thanksgiving for the misfortunes by which God prunes man into fruitfulness; in *The Priesthood* clerics are celebrated as the holy vessels which serve God to the world. The spareness of these titles sets off the richness of the arguments within the poems.

There is a time to be simple and a time to be elaborate. Herbert could be both, and nowhere does this ability manifest itself more fittingly than in the titles of *The Temple.*

4

Time's Pruning Knife:
The Development

ALL OF THE POEMS in "The Church" invite one's admiration and respect; with such neatness has Herbert devised their structures and with such nice tempering of imagination and judgment has he managed their imagery. The uniformly high level of their quality and their thematic variety make *The Temple* the excellent cross section of the life of the spirit that it is; its heterogeneous parts do indeed knit into a coherent whole. And as a whole, it is quite different from Herbert's surviving early verse, both from the several collections of Latin poems and the two English sonnets which he sent to his mother when he was seventeen years old. One has only to compare any sampling of his most famous pieces with any of his immature work to realize that, whereas in *The Temple* he "sounds like Herbert," in the Latin verse he sounds like a proficient but rather anonymous man of letters, and in the New Year's sonnets, as many readers have noticed, he sounds a great deal like his friend Donne. Poetically, Herbert came a long

way between the date of his resolution to devote his talents
to sacred verse and the time that he began the composition
of *The Temple*. Yet he continued to refine his art during
the several years which it took him to complete the volume,
and by a happy chance, we are able to observe the final
evolution of this already accomplished poet. In the eighteenth century, Herbert editors discovered a document
now known as the Williams MS., consisting of a holograph
copy of *Passio Discerpta* and *Lucus,* and, in the hand of an
emanuensis, the sixty-nine earliest poems of *The Temple*.[1]
One can, then, compare the initial core of the volume with
the poems added later. Doing so, he discovers that at least
some of the variety of *The Temple* results from the
differences between the early and late poems. During the
six or seven years or so which he devoted to work on his
volume, Herbert's poetic methods changed. He did not,
of course, completely reverse either his thinking or the
exercise of his craft; interesting differences between the first
and second halves of *The Temple* exist, nevertheless,
differences which are sufficiently cohesive to enable one to
perceive the direction in which Herbert's writing was
moving at the time of his death. Each page of *The Temple*
is distinctively Herbertian, but the Herbert of the last
three or four years of his life was a somewhat different poet
from the man who was yet to move to Bemerton, and a
very different one from the Cambridge orator. Let us
review some of the aspects of his development.

IMAGERY AND INVENTION

IN THE HAND of the Bemerton parson, the image was a
most incisive instrument and of a slightly different order
from his earlier figuration. The distinction consists principally in the way that Herbert came to handle his tropes,
rather than in a shift in their topical range. It is true that
in the latter half of *The Temple* he worked certain kinds

of metaphor more thoroughly than he had before and, at the same time, reduced the frequency of others. Perhaps of some significance is the fact that most of his medical, botanical, and zoological imagery is late, as is that typifying man in terms of architecture, dressing and undressing, and musician or musical instrument; and, on the other hand, most of the figures concerning furniture, astronomy, sports and games, money, legal and commercial matters, and warfare are early. But as I will show presently, these shifts are more indicative of a development in Herbert's conception of the sacred lyric than of alteration in the kind of imagery which he chose to express a given theme. His maturing handling of imagery reveals itself primarily in the rendering of his figurative language, only secondarily in its selection.

Perhaps the clearest illustration of Herbert's increasing skill in the management of his images is the marked difference in the very early and very late treatments of the same figures. In *In S. Scripturas,* the fifth poem in *Lucus,* which Hutchinson dates close to the end of 1623, Herbert characterizes the human heart as a labyrinth:

> Sacratissima Charta, tu fuisti
> Quae cordis latebras sinūsque caecos
> Atque omnes peragrata es angiportus
> Et flexus fugientis appetitûs.
> Ah, quàm docta perambulare calles
> Maeandrósque plicāsque, quàm perita es!
> Quae vis condidit, ipsa nouit aedes. (411)

Trans. O most holy book, you have been in the hidden retreats and blind windings of my heart, and you have searched out every narrow street and fleeting appetite. Ah, how wise you are in traversing the stony ways and winding mazes, how skillful. That power which built the temple, knows it.

In a number of respects, this passage is affinitive to the last lines of *The Pearl*:

> Yet through these labyrinths, not my groveling wit,
> But thy silk twist let down from heav'n to me,
> Did both conduct and teach me, how by it
>   To climbe to thee. (89)

In both poems, the labyrinth is made by God and therefore not inherently evil, though within the heart is *appetitus,* which misused might cause man to desire the wrong goals, just as the possibility exists that the protagonist of *The Pearl* might content himself with the ancillary ways of knowledge, honor, and pleasure. And in both, a way out of the maze is provided by God, through the *sacratissima charta* of the first (surely a pun on chart and book), by means of the silk twist of the later. Yet in three quite important, and for Herbert, typical respects, the later treatment of the metaphor differs from the early one. One is in its extreme economy. In *The Pearl,* Herbert apparently felt that the single word *labyrinths* was enough to suggest all of the architectural features of that structure to his reader, whereas in *Lucus* V he detailed the dark and winding recesses, the meandering paths, the narrow gate, and the like. One word, then, has been entrusted as the equivalent of several lines, and the result is a richer, because more compressed, poetic statement.

In still another respect can we observe Herbert's maturing poetic. In *The Pearl,* both the labyrinth figure and the language with which it is presented are closely integrated with other elements of the poem, whereas in *Lucus* V it stands virtually alone. The labyrinth of *The Pearl* is the complex of the *wayes* of learning, honor, and pleasure, already shown to be opposed in some manner to love of God; one of these ways, pleasure, is chiefly concerned with love and wit (line 24); the fact that this wit is condemned as *groveling* clarifies the nature of the opposition; man's motion without the aid of the silk twist is downward; only with it can he rise. The later passage reads like a Herbert poem and would, I suspect, even were it not so familiar. Its compression, its refusal to be intelligibly detached from context, its heavy reliance on implication as well as direct statement (we do not have the twist patly identified), and the simultaneous simplicity of phrasing—these are the qualities which one associates with the poems of *The Temple,* qualities which Herbert only gradually learned to achieve in his verse.

Let me mention some other instances of Herbert's reworking of an image in the interest of brevity and concatenation. In *Musae Responsoriae* VIII (ca. 1620), he chides Andrew Melville for his irresponsible charge of rampant pride and hypocrisy in the two universities, concluding with the figure of the telescope:

> Quisquis tuetur perspicillis Belgicis
>   Quâ parte tractari solent,
> Res ampliantur, sin per aduersam videt,
>   Minora fiunt omnia:
> Tu qui superbos caeteros existimas
>   (Superbius cùm te nihil)
> Vertas specillum: nam, prout se res habent,
>   Vitro minùs rectè vteris. (388)

Trans. Whoever looks through Belgian perspectives, and holds them in the customary manner, finds that things are magnified; if, however, he looks through the opposite end, everything becomes smaller. You, who judge others to be proud (none prouder than you), turn the telescope: for as things now are, you are using the glass incorrectly.

One's opinion of the size of another's pride depends upon the end of the perspective that he chooses. Several years later, he employed the same metaphor in *Charms and Knots* with greater frugality of expression: "The world thinks all things bigg and tall / Grace turnes ye Optick, then they fall." (97) It is, however, in the last line of *Sinne* (II) that infinitely more subtle use is made of the same trope:

O that I could a sinne once see!
We paint the devil foul, yet he
Hath some good in him, all agree.
Sinne is flat opposite to th' Almighty, seeing
It wants the good of *vertue,* and of *being.*

But God more care of us hath had:
If apparitions make us sad,
By sight of sinne we should grow mad.
Yet as in sleep we see foul death, and live:
So devils are our sinnes in perspective. (63)

In the Latin poem, Herbert makes the reader realize the
sense of largeness and smallness of the image seen through
the glass by supplying several details about the manual
process of reversing the instrument. But there, the association with another motif, the dream of death, ripens the
figure into real fruition. Just as the deaths which we see in
dreams are *apparitions,* visions which have no *being* but
which give some idea of the large state of actual death, God
protects us from direct sight of our own sin, the enormity
of which we could not bear face to face, by allowing us to
see devils, our sin in a different size scale. Herbert avails
himself of not one, but two, characteristics of telescope-
gazing: the magnification, and the fact that it is a particularly unusual kind of looking—most felicitously likened to
what one perceives in a dream. Herbert has, clearly, come
a long way with the telescope.

De Musica Sacra, one of the truly excellent poems in
Musae Responsoriae (XXIII of the series), deserves careful
notice from every reader of Herbert. Two of its stanzas,
seven and nine, form the nucleus of the *Church-musick* of
The Temple, and in the poet's reworking of them one can
clearly see the tendency of the mature Herbert to combine
images and to operate with several at once.

Tu Diua miro pollice spiritum
Caeno profani corporis exuens

Ter millies coelo reponis:
   Astra rogant, Nouus hic quis hospes?

.   .   .   .   .

Quid hocce? Psalmos audion'? o dapes!
O succulenti balsama spiritûs!
   Ramenta coeli, guttulaéque
      Deciduae melioris orbis! (394)

Trans. You, Goddess, with marvelous thumb freeing the
   spirit from the dirt of the profane body, restore it
   to heaven three thousand times. Stars ask, who is
   this new visitor? . . . What is this? Do I hear
   psalms? O solemn feasts! O delicious balms of the
   spirit! fragments of heaven, and falling droplets of
   a better world!

Here are three ideas (though they are separated by a
stanza noting Moses' use of music to arouse his men to
praise of God): music releases the soul from the body; it
allows the soul to reside in heaven; it is a heavenly food.
Several years later, when he composed *Church-musick,*
Herbert expanded two of these elements, and compressed
the third while combining it with the other two:

Sweetest of sweets, I thank you: when displeasure
      Did through my bodie wound my minde,
You took me thence, and in your house of pleasure
      A daintie lodging me assign'd.

Now I in you without a bodie move,
      Rising and falling with your wings:
We both together sweetly live and love,
      Yet say sometimes, *God help poore Kings.*

Comfort, I'le die; for if you poste from me,
      Sure I shall do so, and much more:
But if I travell in your companie,
      You know the way to heavens doore. (65-66)

The pathway to heaven is here more explicitly charted.
In the first stanza, *sweetest of sweets* replaces the more

detailed Latin description of music as heavenly manna
without, I feel, losing any of the richness of suggestion;
here, also, the listener is both fed and housed in music's
house of pleasure, an association not made in the earlier
piece. In the second strophe, his disembodiment is stressed
to the point that the reader realizes that church music is
angelic. It has wings; in it, the protagonist, like an angel,
can move and perceive incorporeally, as sheer harmony
(*rising and falling,* of course, is equally appropriate as
designation of the melodic line and of the flying motion
of the angels). The conclusion presents the inevitable
culmination: traveling in the *companie* of music, he
approaches the very door of heaven, with the word *companie,* and with the implied motif of angels, suggesting
the Preface to the *Sanctus* in the Order for Holy Communion: "Therefore with Angels and Archangels, and with
all the holy company of heaven, we laud and magnify thy
glorious name, evermore praising thee and saying, Holy,
Holy, Holy." From the somewhat general idea of the
heavenly nature of music in *De Musica Sacra,* Herbert has
developed the quite precise course of being fed and lodged
with pleasure, then of his soul leaving his body and
becoming united with that of angels, and finally of being
borne by this company of heaven to their own home. The
conception is more clearly defined, though conveyed through
implication rather than statement and description.

One could profitably examine many other pairs of early
and late poems containing the same image.[2] Perhaps, however, it might be as well to regard Herbert's sharpening of
his tropes from another viewpoint, that of his revisions.
Most of the redactions in the Williams MS. are in Herbert's
own handwriting and thus constitute unquestionable evidence of his growing concern with metaphorical precision
and orderliness. These revisions are not extensive, for the
most part consisting of a change of phrase here, the alteration of a word there. Yet one can discern in nearly all of

them his search for *le mot juste,* either for the language
which would express his meaning more accurately, or for a
word which would sustain the pervading imagery of the
passage. In *The Church-porch,* for example, he tightens his
censure of one's wandering attention in church from "Who
marks in church-time others comlines / Turns all their
beauty to his vglines" to "Who marks in church-time others
symmetrie, / Makes all their beautie his deformitie." (23)
In the initial version of *Easter-wings,* the first stanza concludes "[O let me] sing this day thy sacrifice / Then shall
my fall further the flight in me." (43) Most fittingly,
sacrifice gives way to *victories* (sacrifice is more appropriate
for a Good Friday meditation than for an Easter poem),
and *my* is changed to *the,* an alteration which points
strongly to the doctrine of the Fortunate Fall which is the
real object of the poem. Sustaining of metaphor accounts
for the revision of the final stanza of *Employment* (I), of
which the first version is

> I am no link of thy great chain,
> But all my companie is a weed.
> Lord that I may the Sunns perfection gaine
> Give mee his speed.

In the second, he prays for chain to become musical consort
and weed to become pen:

> I am no link of thy great chain,
> But all my companie is a weed.
> Lord place me in thy consort; give one straine
> To my poore reed. (57)

Herbert petitions in the original conclusion of *Deniall* for
God's favors to chime with his mind and *meet* his rhyme.
For his devotions to be thus assisted by God's countering
his *bent thoughts* is a natural enough wish; but the later
substitution of *mend* for *meet* changes the line from one of
logical soundness to one of poetic brilliance. For his verses

have been likened throughout the poem to two articles
flawed and so in need of repair, a brittle bow and an
untuned and unstrung musical instrument. *Mend,* then,
aligns these metaphors with the request for assistance. In
Christmas, Herbert expresses regret that the Christ child,
the "glorious yet contracted light," should have to be
housed in so lowly an object as a manger. He offers his
soul instead: "ffurnish my soule to thee, y^t being drest /
Of better lodging thou maist be possest." In the revision,
however, he introduces the idea of Easter as the completion
of Christmas and so as its ultimate significance: "Furnish
& deck my soul, that thou mayst have / A better lodging
then a rack or grave." (81) Christmas is hereby assigned
its proper place in the Christian year.

These revisions, and the others which might be cited,
show (as do his more effective uses of the same image in
successive poems) his increasingly sure grasp of accuracy,
metaphorical tightness, and concentration of idea. One can
also track Herbert's development in his gradual retreat
from the simile.[3] A writer using this figure makes a different poetic commitment from the one using the metaphor
and creates a vastly different effect. For the simile is
conspicuously artificial, and by employing it, the poet calls
attention to the fact that the likeness which he draws is at
most tentative—either not to be taken literally by either
poet or reader, or to be regarded as referring only to highly
selective qualities of the things compared. The simile
creates a greater distance between tenor and vehicle than
does even the most contrived metaphor. When it is long
and elaborate, it serves to divert the reader from the
primary subject at hand, and he feels a sense of return to
the norm at its conclusion. Coming upon a simile he is,
I feel, more conscious of being in the presence of figurative
language than he is when he reads a passage containing
other kinds of tropes. Herbert was exceptionally sparing
in his use of similes. They occur, on the average, only once
in every 39.3 lines in *The Temple,* a rare frequency indeed

in verse of such high figurative concentration. This is an even smaller proportion than one finds in Donne, where the typical simile appears every 19.9 lines in *Songs and Sonets,* every 15.0 lines in the anniversaries, and every 14.5 lines in the divine poems. Herbert's similes are, moreover, introduced far more unobtrusively into the verse than Donne's. Donne apparently enjoyed devising lengthy ones and placing them in conspicuous positions. Recall, for example, the conclusion of *Aire and Angels*:

> Then as an Angell, face, and wings
> Of aire, not pure as it, yet pure doth weare,
> So thy love may be my loves spheare:
> Just such disparitie
> As is twixt Aire and Angells puritie,
> 'Twixt womens love, and mens will ever bee.

Or that of *The Flea*: "Just so much honor, when thou yeeld'st to mee, / Will wast, as this flea's death tooke life from thee." Or the beginning of *A Valediction: Forbidding Mourning:*

> As virtuous men passe mildly away,
> And whisper to their soules, to goe,
> Whilst some of their sad friends doe say,
> The breath goes now, and some say, no:
> So let us melt, and make no noise. . . .

Or that of *The Extasie*:

> Where, like a pillow on a bed,
> A pregnant banke swel'd up, to rest
> The violets reclining head,
> Sat we two, one anothers best.

Frequently Donne marks the climax of an argument with a memorable simile, or points up logical transitions with the trope. He seems anxious to call attention to his figures as figures.

Herbert, however, regularly integrates his similes quite

smoothly into the verse. In *Christmas,* for example, he writes

> I will go searching, till I finde a sunne
>   Shall stay, till we have done;
> A willing shiner, that shall shine as gladly,
>   As frost-nipt sunnes look sadly. (81)

The simile is short; it embellishes a previous figure of speech, the metaphor of Christ as the sun. It does not "stand out" as do most of Donne's. And this is a typical passage. Again and again, his similes enlarge upon a more conspicuous figure. So in *Praise* (III):

>   . . . When mine eyes
> Did weep to heav'n, they found a bottle there
>   (As we have boxes for the poore)
> Readie to take them in. . . . (158)

And in *The Invitation*: "Here is joy that drowneth quite / Your delight, / As a floud the lower grounds." (180) Sometimes, Herbert dissipates the novelty of the simile either by continuing its imagery in the following lines or by insisting on a near literal interpretation of something in it which at first appears fanciful. In *The Starre,* one is likely to think initially of the bee simile as merely a rather precious way of expressing the poet's wish to fly to heaven:

> Sure thou wilt joy, by gaining me
>   To flie home like a laden bee
>   Unto that hive of beams
>   And garland streams. (74)

By the time that he has completed the stanza, however, one sees that Herbert seriously associates Heaven and a beehive, and so the only figurative quantity peculiar to the simile is that the bee is *laden*. The phrase coheres firmly with the surrounding metaphors.

Herbert was, in short, chary with his similes and

blended the ones he used evenly with the other, more positive tropes. Both of these characteristics became more pronounced in his verse as he matured. In the Williams MS., the typical simile occurs every 34.2 lines, whereas in the later poems, the frequency drops to one every 46.0 lines. Or perhaps, since "The Church-porch" and "The Church Militant" have no counterpart among the late work, a more valid comparison would be that of the Williams poems of "The Church" and the subsequent additions. The early poems in "The Church" contain one simile per 26.7 lines, as opposed to the late average of one in 46.0. A notable quality of Herbert's development, then, is the sharp decrease in the rate of occurrence of his similes and a corresponding reliance upon figures which blend more smoothly into the milieu of the verse.

Herbert's distinctive manner of naming his poems emerged only gradually. The individual sections of *Musae Responsoriae, Passio Discerpta, Lucus,* and *Alia Poemata Latina* bear headings which quite straightforwardly indicate the subjects to be treated; those of *Memoriae Matris Sacrum* are untitled. The large majority of the captions in the Williams MS. are eminently direct. Scanning them, one finds clear guideposts like *The Altar, Easter, H. Baptisme, Love, Church-musick, Imploiment, Sinn, Praise, Ungratfulnes, The World, Prayer, Death, Iudgment, Heaven.* A handful, however, indicate that Herbert was beginning to discover the kind of designation which characterizes his last work, one which does not merely signal a theme, but which metaphorically adds dimension to the poem to which it is attached. Three of the "new" kind of titles are chosen with an obvious eye to involving the three poems in the image of the temple. "The Church-porch," "Perirranterium," and *Superliminare* are named so that the reader realizes that Herbert's volume will conduct him on a figurative tour through a place of worship (and thus he is prepared for the nature of much of the content); at the same time that the titles enrich the central metaphor of the whole, they add to the value of the poems which they head. For the recipe for ethical responsibility to be called "The Church-porch" shows it to be inferior to spiritual quickness, though decency is prerequisite to holiness; the title of *Superliminare* casts it as an evaluation of who should enter the temple. Two other early poems invite our particular attention. *Jordan* (I) was always called thus, and *The Pearl* apparently bore this name from the beginning, though in the Williams MS. Herbert did not append the explanatory *Matth. 13.45* which, appearing in the Bodleian MS. and in the early editions, was perhaps added to insure the reader's grasp of the contribution which the Biblical allusion makes to the final stanza. These five names, then, operate in far more complex fashion than any of those of the other early work.

When one compares the headings of the Williams MS. and those in the remainder of the little book which reached the hands of Nicholas Ferrar, he finds two principal differences. Most salient is the high incidence of metaphorical titles among the late poems. *Sighs and Grones, Vertue, Home, The Quip, Love-joy, The Bunch of Grapes, Mans Medley, Paradise, Divinitie, The Familie, The Size, Artillerie, The Discharge, The Holdfast, The Bag, The Jews, The Collar, Clasping of hands, Josephs coat, The Pulley, The Crosse, The Sonne, The Water-course, The Glance, Aaron, The Foil, The Forerunners,* and *A Parodie*: all are newcomers to the canon, and the titles of all effect some special communication, either an enriching ambiguity, or the suggestion of a motif which qualifies the materials of the text itself. By naming these pieces as he did, Herbert endowed them with a magnitude of statement which they would lack if more simply styled.

The second difference between the early and late titles affords us a glimpse of Herbert in the process of selecting his titles. Eight of the poems in the Williams MS. were retitled by the time they were copied at Little Gidding, all but one in the interest of infusing additional meaning. That one, originally designated *Tentation,* is the poem which we know as *Affliction* (IV) *(Broken in pieces all asunder).* We cannot, of course, assign the change to a definite cause. Perhaps Herbert intended it to associate the mode of temptation treated here, that of one's own rebellious thoughts, with those of the other affliction poems —illness in *Affliction* (I), awareness of one's unworthiness in *Affliction* (II), grief which shows man his affinity to Christ in *Affliction* (III), and the vicissitudes of all men after Adam which, properly undergone, make him stronger than the first man in *Affliction* (V)—and so to make the group a five-part complement commenting on human calamity. One simply cannot be sure. The reasons for the other changes, however, are easier to estimate. *The Second Thanksgiving* becomes *The Reprisall,* forming an extension of the military and musical imagery of its predecessor, *The Thanksgiving.* The sonnet in the Passiontide section now bearing the name *Redemption* was originally called *The Passion;* the altered designation nicely points up the legal imagery, at the same time furnishing a more accurate implication of one of the values of the Crucifixion, deliverance from the worldly places enumerated in the third quatrain. *The Quidditie* was initially called *Poetry.* By substituting the more specific word for the general one, Herbert appreciably deepened the poem. Verse, the new title indicates, is for Herbert the essence of life, through which he is most with God. But in its popular Renaissance sense, a quiddity was a sophistic haggle, and so the relativity of the value of the much touted worldly pleasures catalogued in the first two stanzas (hawking, banqueting, dancing, and so on) is but a specious quibble. The poem now styled *Jordan* (II) started out as *Invention,* its heading merely picking up the subject announced in the first three lines ("When first my lines of heav'nly joyes made mention / . . . I sought out

quaint words, and trim invention"). The new title couples
this denunciation of Herbert's own early poetic artificiality
with that of the secular poets called to account in *Jordan*
(I), showing him to be but one degree better because he at
least chose the worthiest of subjects. *Miserie* appears in
the Williams MS. as *The Publican*. Herbert doubtless
realized the faultiness of this early metaphorical title, saw
that the foolish and dull-spirited man anatomized in the
poem was far more nearly universal in type than the New
Testament tax collector undeniably suggested by the word
publican. Wisely, he substituted *Miserie*, and in so doing,
strengthened the poem, for the final name shows the reader
something which the blind worldling of the poem fails to
see: that all of his stubborn self-indulgence can lead only
to distress and misery.

Perhaps the most interesting, and the most informative,
of all the title changes are those of *Church-lock and key*
and *The Elixir*, which accompany substantial revisions of
the poems. *Church-lock and key*, the twenty-fifth poem in
the Williams MS., was named *Prayer*. Herbert seemingly
did not associate it with either of the early poems treating
material aspects of the church, *Church-Musick* and *Church-
Monuments*, which occupied the twentieth and fortieth
position. Neither of these, it should be observed, are
allegories; real music is praised because it quickens the
spirit, and actual monuments provide the occasion for a
meditation on death and physical dissolution. In the
Bodleian MS., the two have been drawn together and two
more church-property verses have been added, *The Church-
floore* and *The Windows*. But neither deals with a literal
part of the building. In *The Church-floore* the true object
of examination is the human heart and its impulses of
patience, humility, confidence, and charity; the windows of
the other poem are correlatives for the priest, who, with
the doctrines of the church fixed within his soul as colored
images are annealed in stained glass, shines through a wider

spectrum than does the profane man. To this group of four church poems, the two old and the two new, Herbert adds a transformed version of *Prayer*. Originally it began thus:

> I know it is my sinne, which stops thine eares,
> > And bindes thy hands,
> Out-crying my requests, drowning my tears;
> Or else the chilnesse of my faint demands. (66)

Two simple emendations suit it for inclusion in the new group. *Stops* in the first line is cancelled in favor of *locks,* and the title is changed to *Church-lock and key*. The claim for prayer is made stronger by the new metaphor, particularly in view of the double meaning of *church* urged by *The Church-floore*. Prayer not only unlocks God's ears but opens the human heart.

   A similar transmutation occurs in *Perfection,* which argued that the most contaminated of men could avail himself of God's perfection and become pure. The only hint of chemical imagery occurred in the present fourth stanza:

> All may of thee partake:
> Nothing can be so low,
> Which with his tincture (for thy sake)
> Will not to Heauen grow. (184)

His imagination apparently fired by *tincture,* Herbert extended the implications by rewriting the stanza:

> All may of thee partake:
> Nothing can be so mean,
> Which with his tincture (for thy sake)
> Will not grow bright and clean.

He struck out the original fourth stanza, where the imagery of the devil was at odds with the new alchemical figure, and substituted for a concluding stanza embellished with light imagery, the present ending:

> This is the famous stone
> That turneth all to gold:
> For that which God doth touch and own
> Cannot for lesse be told.

He called the revised product *The Elixir,* and infinitely improved it is.

Several of the characteristics which we have been surveying—the nature of Herbert's revisions, his increasingly fine discipline of his imagery, and his progressive shifting from literal to metaphorical titles—suggest a gradual change in his conception of the devotional lyric. And when one examines the early and late sections of *The Temple,* he does indeed find that the two groups contain different *kinds* of poems. Different management of imagery, then, is closely involved in the production of a quite different type of verse. Poetic manner can, after all, scarcely differ completely from matter. Surely in Herbert's work, invention and figuration keep pace.

He abandoned some of the practices evident in the Williams MS. For one thing, he did not continue to write long poems like *The Church-porch, The Sacrifice,* and *The Church Militant.* All are good-sized—463, 253, and 279 lines, respectively. *Providence,* their only near counterpart among the late poems (152 lines), is considerably shorter. Since the three early poems represent such divergent types, I think one must conclude that he turned from their length, not their genera. At the same time, he began writing more extremely short poems, almost miniatures. The only poems in the Williams MS. of less than sonnet length are *Superliminare* (eight lines), *Sinne* (II) (ten), *Trinitie Sunday* (the inevitable nine), *Coloss. iii.3* (ten), and *A Wreath* (twelve). A larger number appear among the late poems: *Anagram* (one couplet), *Justice* (I) (twelve lines), *Jesu* (ten), *Love-joy* (eight), *Hope* (eight), *The Jews* (twelve), *The Call* (twelve), *Dialogue-Anthem* (ten), *The Watercourse* (ten), *Bitter-sweet* (eight), *The Foil* (eight) and *The*

Posie (twelve). These very short poems are short because they are all the blossoming of a single metaphor—the army-Mary permutation in the first, the variations of one sentence in *Justice* (I), the discovery of the meaning of the name in the third, the explanation of the window-glass in the third, the explanation of the acrostic in *Love-joy,* the exchange of tokens with Hope, the wish to mend the aridity of contemporary Judaism, the invocation of God in triads of attributive names, Christian's repudiation of Death in the rhetoric of the Office of the Burial of the Dead, man's choice between the course of heaven and the course of earth, the characterization of one's days as sweet and sour, the metaphor of the foil, and the defense of the simple motto in *The Posie.* Each of the poems, then, is one carefully and imaginatively rendered image, suggestive of an abundant range of experience, slight only in number of lines.

Herbert's most famous pattern poems, *The Altar* and *Easter-wings,* were both composed by the time the Williams MS. was copied. Because they are his sole ventures in shaping the verse into a silhouette of the subject treated, he must have made a choice not to delineate other visual forms. These two, of course, were motivated in part by his wish to Christianize a patently classical genre, and the altars and wings of the *Greek Anthology* provided ideal subjects for this treatment. Had he so desired, however, he could have baptized some of the other picture poems in the *Anthology.* His attraction to the theme of Christ's gentling the Lord of Hosts might well have recommended the ax to him; the bow and arrow seems a natural shape for one fond of alluding to the darts of divine love; he could well have used the pipes of Pan as the basis for one of his many musical poems; his repeated association of the soul and newly-hatched birds might have made him consider making an egg-shaped poem. Or, had he felt inclined to go beyond the Greek models, he would have found an abundance of

Christian symbols easily imitated—crosses, circles, and tri-
angles, for example. Seemingly, he decided against further
pictorial representation. He did, however, continue the
visual suggestion with which he had experimented in the
germinal poems of *The Temple*. There one finds *Deniall*,
its imperfect rhymes mended in the concluding stanza,
though here the appeal is to the ear as well as to the mind
and eye; *Coloss. iii.3*, within each line of which is "hidden"
one of the words of the verse *(My life is hid in Him that is
my treasure)*; *Antiphon* (II), in which the praise for God's
joining the ranks of men and angels is dramatized by the
consolidation of their rhymes in the final strophe; and *A
Wreath*, which, by means of a circular rhyme pattern
*(praise, give, wayes, live, straight, thee, deceit, simplicitie,
live, wayes, give, Praise)* and anadiplosis, materially suggests its subject.

Among the later poems, one finds a substantial number
of this type. In *Ana-* $\begin{Bmatrix} \text{MARY} \\ \text{ARMY} \end{Bmatrix}$ *gram* Herbert almost graphi-
cally renders the Virgin's pregnancy ("How well her name
an *Army* doth present, / in whom the *Lord of Hosts* did
pitch his tent!"); in *Dialogue*, Herbert and God speak in
alternate stanzas, the existence of the dialogue being
emphasized by the italicizing of God's lines; the unrhymed
last line of *Grief* signals the discord occasioned by that
emotion; Herbert tracks the double motion of sin in *Sinnes
round* by means of a system of word repetitions; it moves
one in circles, and so the first and last lines of the poem
are identical; at the same time, it builds a structure three
stories high, a performance suggested by the second and
third stanzas beginning with a repetition of the concluding
line of the preceding strophe. In *Clasping of hands* Herbert
furnishes visible token of the joining through exceptionally
heavy word repetitions (only fifty-three different words
occur in the twenty lines) and through the interlacing of
the rhyme words *(thine, more, mine, restore, mind, more,*

thine, restore, mine, thine; mine, more, thine, restore, mine more, thine, restore, thine, Mine). Praise (III), which opens with Herbert's promise to spin God's praise forever, contains a hint of the spiritual spinning wheel's motion in its complementary rhymes at the conclusion of each stanza *(store-more, before-more, doore-more, shore-more, poore-more, sore-more, store-more).* The exact parallel of those of the first and last stanzas, and some internal verbal repetitions in addition, make the wheel describe a full circle. The endings of the two stanzas of *The Water-course* are probably intended to look like the subject, though their effect is minimized by the conventional stanzas which they conclude:

> For who can look for lesse, that loveth $\begin{cases} \text{Life?} \\ \text{Strife?} \end{cases}$
>
> Who gives to man, as he sees fit, $\begin{cases} \text{Salvation.} \\ \text{Damnation.} \end{cases}$ (170)

And finally *Paradise,* a defense of God's testing and disciplining of man, operates in terms of the imagery of skillfully pruned trees. The reader actually sees the pruning because the rhyme words of each tercet, printed in capital letters, form a sequence of diminution: GROW-ROW-OW, CHARM-HARM-ARM, START-TART-ART, SPARE-PARE-ARE, FREND-REND-END.

Herbert let the absolute hieroglyph rest, then, when he completed *The Altar* and *Easter-wings,* but he continued with visual half-mimesis during the last three years of his life, producing a growing number of verses graced by the device. Herbert's moving in this direction parallels, I think, the course taken by his management of imagery and idea. Just as he moved gradually from direct and detailed statement to implication and intimation, he forsook poems which looked exactly like some object in favor of those which only suggested it. The two pathways led to the same destination.

One of the most important distinctions between the early and late poems is the marked difference between the kinds of dramatic situations which they establish. In the majority of the Williams MS. poems, fifty-three of the seventy-eight, Herbert addresses God directly, surely the most natural and the most widespread mode of devotional verse, and that which he would have found most frequently in the meditations of his own countrymen. While these fifty-three range through a multiplicity of psychological states, modulating from the serenity of *Easter* through the sensitive confession of *Ungratefulnesse* to the near-despair of *Deniall,* they nevertheless share a uniformity: all are prayers of a sort; the reader examining them is a definite outsider, not immediately involved by the *persona* of the verse in the problem at hand. He is, in a sense, a privileged eavesdropper, allowed limited access to a firmly circumscribed monologue directed above. He plays no direct role. Of the ninety-five late poems in *The Temple,* however, only forty are framed as speeches to God. The greater number institute a closer relationship between poet and reader than do the petitions which constitute the bulk of the earlier work. And at the same time, they specify a far greater variety of settings and situations than one finds in the Williams MS. material.

Only in the two opening poems of the initial version of *The Temple* does Herbert directly address another person; he explains to the reader, the visitor to the temple, the conditions which he must meet in order to enter. Yet neither poem succeeds in involving the general reader in a close association with it or with the poet; impersonality prevails despite the mode of speech. Most readers are proscribed by the opening words of "The Church-porch":

> Thou, whose sweet youth and early hopes inhance
> Thy rate and price, and mark thee for a treasure;
> Hearken unto a Verser, who may chance
> Rhyme thee to good, and make a bait of pleasure. (6)

And the highly stylized formula of the *Superliminare* invites no intimacy: "Thou, whom the former precepts have / Sprinkled and taught, how to behave / Thy self in church. . . ." (25) In a substantial number of the later poems, however, Herbert assumes a more specific human audience, speaking in such a manner as to draw the reader into the poem. This interior view of the verse does much to relieve the matter-of-fact allegory of *The Church-floore*:

> Mark you the floore? that square & speckled stone,
>> Which looks so firm and strong,
>>> Is *Patience:*

> And th' other black and grave, wherewith each one
>> Is checker'd all along,
>>> *Humilitie:*

> The gentle rising, which on either hand
>> Leads to the Quire above,
>>> Is *Confidence:*

> But the sweet cement, which in one sure band
>> Ties the whole frame, is *Love*
>>> And *Charitie.* (66-67)

Without the stage directions describing the four parts of the floor, directions which particularly compel the reader because they are directed *to him,* this part of the poem would consist of four quite bare equations. And were they stated as such, they would fail to withstand much scrutiny, for though the intrinsic properties of the rise make it suitable to emblemize confidence, and though the cohesive quality of the cement enables one to accept it as charity, the colors of the patience and humility stones seem to have nothing to do with their symbolism. The dressing of the reader-involvement, nevertheless, is cleverly managed to blur this inexactness.

The reader is drawn into the poem in *Vanitie* (I), equally skillfully, but for different reasons. Here Herbert divides humanity into two categories: *man,* exemplified by

the destructive and appetitive searchers of the first three
stanzas; and we, Herbert and the reader, who is thus
subtly urged to become part of the *we*:

> What hath not man sought out and found,
> But his deare God? who yet his glorious law
> Embosomes in us, mellowing the ground
>   With showres and frosts, with love & aw,
> So that we need not say, Where's this command?
>   Poore man, thou searchest round
> To finde out *death,* but missest *life* at hand. (85-86)

By the time that one has reached the last two lines he is
anxious *not* to be the one spoken to.

With consummate tenderness, but nevertheless with
bluntness, Herbert designates the reader as *poore silly soul*
in *Vanitie* (II), *foolish soul who sinn'd today* in *Businesse,*
foolish man in *Divinitie;* that the reader recognizes himself as such is one of the ingredients of the success of these
poems. The "Thou who condemnest Jewish hate / for
choosing Barrabas a murderer / before the Lord of glorie"
of *Self-condemnation* is shown to be worse, "a Judas-Jew,"
since he prefers the false gold of the world before the true
of heaven. Doubtless the second, and invisible, person of
Assurance is not intended as the reader; whoever he is, he
draws Herbert out of the framework of his private meditations:

>   O spitefull bitter thought!
> Bitterly spitefull thought! Couldst thou invent
> So high a torture? Is such poyson bought?
> Doubtlesse, but in the way of punishment.
>   When wit contrives to meet with thee,
>   No such rank poyson can there be.
>
>   Thou said'st but even now,
> That all was not so fair, as I conceiv'd,
> Betwixt my God and me. . . . (155)

The second person of *An Offering,* while frankly shadowy, precipitates the poem into a little human drama:

> Come, bring thy gift. If blessings were as slow
> As mens returns, what would become of fools?
> What hast thou there? a heart? but is it pure?
> Search well and see; for hearts have many holes. (147)

In his last years Herbert not only addressed an estimable group of poems to a second person; he also conducted dialogues of one with some aspect of his own personality. In only three of the early poems does he do this. He speaks to his heart in *Easter* ("Rise heart; thy Lord is risen"); to his body in *Church-monuments* ("Deare flesh, while I do pray, learn here thy stemme / And true descent"); to his thoughts in *Content* ("Peace mutt'ring thoughts, and do not grudge"). But later, apparently pleased with the dramatic quality effected by this device, he employed it more frequently. In *Conscience* he turns to that faculty ("Peace pratler, do not lowre"); in *The Dawning,* to his heart ("Awake sad heart, whom sorrow ever drowns"); again to his heart in *The Method* ("Poore heart, lament"); again in *The Size* ("Content thee, greedie heart"); and in *The Discharge* ("Busie enquiring heart, what wouldst thou know?"); in *The Collar* ("Not so, my heart: but there is fruit, / And thou hast hands"); and to his happiness in *A Parodie* ("Souls joy, when thou art gone").

Increasing numbers of his poems record conversations with abstractions. Only five of the early ones do so— *Church-musick, Sunday, Lent, Death,* and *Heaven.* In the course of expanding *The Temple,* however, Herbert addressed a star, avarice, roses, and daylight, and spring (in *Vertue*), flowers (in *Life*), the British church, providence, hope, time, peace, joy (in *The Bunch of Grapes*), mother church (in *Church-rents and scismes*), justice, despair (in

The Bag), delight (in *The Glimpse*), the elements of the Eucharist (in *The Banquet*), the priesthood, grief, sweet phrases and lovely metaphors (in *The Forerunners*), and invention, comparisons, and wit (in *The Posie*). Complementary to Herbert's moving away from the prayer, then, is the multiplication of the number of poems in which he addresses some other agent—another person, an aspect of himself, an abstraction.

For the poems in which he speaks to God to be displaced by these other types makes it all the more remarkable that it is in the late poems God speaks most often to him. Few literary personages besides Don Camillo have been more comprehensively instructed by the deity than the protagonist of *The Temple,* but it is almost exclusively in Herbert's late verse that the Voice is heard. Among the Williams MS. group Christ is, of course, the locutor of *The Sacrifice,* but the fact that He recounts His abuses while incarnate keeps this poem from exemplifying the God-to-human communication so distinctive in the mature Herbert; *Love* (III) reports a conversation between a devout person and Divine Love, but, since it takes place in Heaven, it, too, fails to be completely typical. Christ speaks at the end of *Redemption,* but to a witness of the Crucifixion. *Jordan* (II) is the only early poem in which Herbert arranges the surprise of having God interrupt his thoughts by breaking into speech, catching him up and giving a clear diagnosis of his error:

> But while I bustled, I might heare a friend
> Whisper, *How wide is all this long pretence!*
> *There is in love a sweetnesse readie penn'd:*
> *Copie out onely that, and save expense.* (103)

Later, however, God speaks to Herbert's narrator a number of times. In *The Collar,* He makes His most famous utterance, at once gently and censoriously calling the fierce and wild raver *Child.* He is assigned alternate stanzas in

Dialogue, chiding His creature for presuming to criticize His great love (*"What, Child, is the ballance thine, | Thine the poise and measure?"*). At the conclusion of *A true Hymne,* He assures the anxious poet: "As when th' heart sayes (sighing to be approved) | *O, could I love!* and stops: God writeth, *Loved.*" (168) At the conclusion of *The Method,* the devotee is promised God's direct commendation when he has achieved proper humility:

> Then once more pray:
> Down with thy knees, up with thy voice
> Seek pardon first, and God will say,
> *Glad heart rejoyce.* (134)

The personage of *Artillerie* is caught up for negligently brushing aside a star, a heavenly messenger, which has fallen into his lap:

> When suddenly I heard one say,
> *Do as thou usest, disobey,*
> *Expell good motions from thy breast,*
> *Which have the face of fire, but end in rest.* (139)

It is probably God who warns Herbert that the end of his pilgrimage is death:

> . . . So I flung away,
>   Yet heard a crie
> Just as I went, *None goes that way*
> *And lives:* If that be all, said I,
> After so foul a journey death is fair,
>   And but a chair. (142)

In *Longing,* the protagonist borders on proud despair, only to be checked by a supernatural admonition:

> Lord Jesu, thou didst bow
> Thy dying head upon the tree:
>   O be not now
>   More dead to me!

Lord heare! *Shall he that made the eare,*
                              Not heare?   (149)

And Christ speaks the two final stanzas of *The Bag,* explaining that, in the absence of luggage, He will use His side-wound to carry messages back to heaven. *The Pulley* probably has as small a claim for membership in this group as *The Sacrifice;* although God speaks all but the first line, which summarizes the creation, He is really musing aloud. Heaven is here speaking to Heaven, not to earth. But speak to earth it does in *The Collar, Dialogue, The Method, Artillerie, Longing,* and *The Bag*—all late poems, paralleled in the Williams MS. only by *Jordan* (II).

Much of the early poetry deals with objects and festivals of the church and with events in human history of particular concern to the church. *Good Friday, Easter, Easter-wings, Whitsunday, Trinitie Sunday, Sunday, Christmas, Lent, Dooms-day, Judgment, H. Baptisme, The H. Communion,* and *Mattens* all fall into the pre-1629 group; the only counterpart among the new poems is *Even-song,* and that poem was composed to replace an *Even-song* paired in the Williams MS. with *Mattens.* Although other events in the Christian year must surely have been attractive to Herbert—Epiphany, Advent, and Ash Wednesday—he did not choose to make them the subjects of whole poems. His later meditations are focused differently. Nor did he center many late poems on physical aspects of the church. *The Church-porch, Superliminare, The Altar, Church-lock and key, Church-monuments, Church-musick,* and *The Knell* far outweigh *The Windows* and *The Church-floore,* which only nominally treat those architectural features. Two of the later poems, *The Crosse* and *Love-joy,* could easily have been formed into reflections on the altar cross and a church window, yet Herbert seems at pains to turn our attention from any one cross in the first, and in the second to keep the location of the window as indefinite as possible.

Herbert's decreasing production of explicitly church-

centered poems is accompanied by an increase in the number set within the purview of everyday life. Only four of
the early ones "take place" in extra-ecclesiastical environ-
ments. In *Jordan* (I) and *Jordan* (II) Herbert addresses an
audience concerned with the proper nature of poetry; in
Humilitie he recounts a fable in which the virtues assemble
around an azure throne; in *The World,* another allegory,
the scene lies in secular history. But a substantial group of
later poems treat lay situations. *Affliction* (III) depicts the
speaker sighing in reverie; the personage of *The Starre* has
just noticed a shooting star; in *Avarice,* he stands before a
heap of coins; in *Vertue,* he contemplates the glories of a
spring day; in *Life,* he regards the bouquet which he has
just gathered; in *Conscience,* he chides that prattler for
souring the pleasures of his day; *The Quip* takes place in a
setting similar to that of *The World;* the protagonist of
Vanitie (II) taxes the silly soul enchanted with the frip-
peries of the world; in *Dulnesse,* he petitions for deliverance
from the sugared lies of the flesh, which make him akin to
the wanton lover; in *Hope,* he exchanges tokens with that
personified virtue; in *Time,* he meets in passing the wielder
of the scythe; in *Love unknown,* he bids his listener sit
down to hear a long and sad tale; in *The Storm,* he muses
on the disturbance before him; in *Artillerie,* sitting before
his cell, he is surprised by a star shooting into his lap; in
The Discharge, he administers a tongue-lashing to his heart,
which has just turned, leered, and looked high and low with
a licorous eye; in *Assurance,* he remonstrates with an
acquaintance who alleges God's indifference; in *Grief,* he
summons all possible aids to weeping—springs, clouds, rain,
running verses; in *The Sonne,* he commends the English
language to his countrymen; in *The Foil,* he is looking at
the heavens; in *The Forerunners,* he has just noticed some
grey hairs in his head; in *The Rose,* he answers a friend
who has urged him to indulge in more worldly pleasures,
handing him a flower as he does so.

In several respects, then, Herbert gives less poetic

attention to man in the church and becomes increasingly occupied with the churchman in the world, though it is always a world which he sees in sacred perspective, one which offers as many inducements to pious contemplation as do the contents of the parish church. Stars, storms, roses, language, his greying hair, conversations with friends, the metal in coins, sensuous attractions—all are made types of divine worship, agents designed to test or to please man. All become the central subjects of poems. This is not to say that in the last years of his life Herbert returned to the kind of homiletics which he had set forth in "The Church-porch." The sermons which he finds in stones are every bit as spiritually oriented as are his meditations on incidents in the life of Christ and his speculations on last things. His whitening hair does not incite him to a prudent old age, but leads him to reflect that the intellect is only accessory to the loving heart. *Avarice* is no repetition of the advice for using money which one finds in the eleventh section of "The Church-porch"; rather it dissects man's propensity to revere false symbols, even those which he has himself stamped with a human face. *Time* does not enjoin one to use his time wisely, but affirms how little man need fear time and death since the coming of Christ. The mature Herbert found ontological reminders at every turn, not alone in theological and liturgical materials. From the beginning, of course, he drew upon the imagery of mundane experience to give immediacy and credence to his statements about the spirit. But only in his late verse did he at all regularly deal with the experiences themselves and infuse them with the meditative significance which earlier he had associated primarily with Biblical incidents, ecclesiastical objects, and seasons of the church year.

The various strands of Herbert's development form one cord. The increasingly significant titles are, certainly, only one aspect of his emergent ability to make a single image count for more through finer control of its implications and through its qualification of its companion images. Similarly, his moving from imagerial statement to implication is a counterpart to his foregoing further topiary pieces like *The Altar* and *Easter-wings* in favor of less literal representations like *Anagram* and *The Water-course,* while his expanding apprehension of what the devotional lyric could be led him at once to devise a greater repertory of dramatic situations for his poems and to go outside the precincts of the church in search of meditative paradigms. Had Herbert abandoned work on *The Temple* after drafting the poems of the Williams MS., we would have not only a shorter, but a much less important, volume. We would miss most of the meditations on man's spiritual activity during the last six days of the week, most of the superb reflections on the natural world's mirroring of the deity, many of Herbert's most profound expressions of confidence in God's unfathomable love, many of the excellent qualities of the early poems which came into being only when they were later revised. Even readers who know *The Temple* only through the samplings provided by anthologies (samplings which are remarkably consistent) would miss *The Pulley, Peace, The Collar, The Glance, Antiphon* (I), *Vanitie* (I), *The Bunch of Grapes, Vertue,* and *Discipline,* to name a few of the deservedly favored late poems. And the careful student of the seventeenth century, in addition to missing these and other pieces of comparable quality, would, in the absence of the last poems of *The Temple,* adjudge Herbert's performance as brilliant but narrow. Some of his most precise and subtle imagery, and much of his thematic variety, is to be found in the production of his final years.

PROSODY

HERBERT'S MASTERY of versification has long been an academic and even popular byword. College sophomores are informed of his skill, and almost every scholarly contribution to our understanding of his poetry includes some notice of his gifts as a craftsman. And rightly so, for the plenitude of his stanzaic invention constitutes no small portion of his art; and, far from being a mere display of ingenuity, it functions as accessory to his thematic expression. My concern here is not with adding to the general esteem in which Herbert's prosodical talents are held, for that is scarcely necessary, but with indicating some of the mutations which his practice underwent during the composition of *The Temple,* mutations which, like the changes in his management of imagery, evince his steady pursuit of precision and concentration of idea. His close attention to form began early, as a glance at the Latin poems reveals, and so a comparison of the early and late pieces of *The Temple* does not show him learning to shape verse. This, he could do well when he began his volume; and he had, apparently, already fixed many of his formal precepts, so that one finds more similarities than differences between the first and last poems. The whole *Temple* is, of course, pervaded by stanzaic variety. In both groups of poems, moreover, he consistently uses the iambic foot; in neither does he make a verse line of more than five stresses; his enjambed lines are uniformly rare; never does he sustain a stanza pattern like *abcd* in which some lines have no rhyme counterparts; from the beginning he appears to have preferred cross rhymes to enclosed ones; also from the beginning, he delighted in devising stanzas including lines of sharply contrasting lengths.

Herbert manifests, then, a stability of technique in the six- or seven-year period represented by the poems in *The Temple.* Yet this stability is far from stasis: he did not exercise his metrical acuity solely in contriving additional stanza designs; in addition he found new ways to make cleaner articulations of his ideas. In several ways, he tightened the framework of his stanzas. Some time ago

Albert McHarg Hayes observed a characteristic of Herbert's structure which he christened *counterpoint,* an arrangement whereby the rhyming lines of a given stanza are of different lengths, while the lines of identical lengths do not rhyme.[4] While one might question the value of some of Hayes' five gradations between wholly harmonic and wholly contrapuntal forms,[5] his conclusion is valid and, I think, important: much more frequently than the poets customarily associated with him (Donne, Crashaw, Marvell, Vaughan, and Traherne), Herbert imposed formal coherence on his stanzas by using line lengths as well as rhymes to suggest affinity between lines. Thus the pattern of *Content* (*a*5, *b*4, *a*5, *a*4) is at once less interesting and less unified than that of *Vanitie* (I) (*a*4, *b*5, *a*5, *b*4, *c*5, *a*3, *c*5), where the lines that *look* alike, because of Herbert's scheme of indenting, are associated with others by rhymes. Of particular concern here is the fact that the majority of the poems with "counterpoint" are late: only nineteen, or forty-seven percent, of the Williams pieces contain it, whereas forty-four, or sixty-four percent, of the late poems are contrapuntal. Most poems of the Bemerton period, then, benefit from this type of stanzaic integration.

Such integration worked with other poetic adhesives to enable Herbert to manage longer and more elaborate stanzas. Almost half of the stanzaic poems of the Williams MS., twenty-three of the fifty-nine, are written in quatrains. There is, of course, nothing at all wrong with a four-line stanza. Strophic brevity can be a genuine asset, as the success of *Vertue* and *Bitter-sweet* and *Discipline* (all late poems) proves. The quatrain has served many poets well indeed. Yet had Herbert continued to rely heavily on a unit of four lines, *The Temple* would not be the landmark of formal variety that it is. He did not, fortunately. Rather he used increasing numbers of longer stanzas, which, while substantially more complex than the quatrain, nonetheless maintain their unity. A bare idea of the extent of his late innovation can be gained from a formulaic comparison:

Williams MS. Poems		New *Temple* Poems	
6-line stanzas:		6-line stanzas:	
14 poems	*ababcc*	32 poems	*ababcc*
	aabbcc		*abbacc*
	aabccb		*abcbca*
	abccba		*aabccb*
	abbacc		*abacbc*
	abcabc		*ababcb*
	ababab		*abaccb*
			abcbac
			abcabc
7-line stanzas:		7-line stanzas:	
1 poem	*ababcac*	3 poems	*ababcac*
			ababbcc
			ababccb
8-line stanzas:		8-line stanzas:	
2 poems	*ababccdd*	6 poems	*aaabcccb*
	ababcdcd		*aabccbdd*
			ababccdd
			ababccc
			abacbddc

It should be noticed that Herbert arranges the rhyme sequences in most of the late poems so that the stanzas do not tend to divide themselves into two sub-stanzas. The distribution of the *b*-rhymes in *aabccbdd,* for example, prevents this design's resembling two loosely joined quatrains; the same is true of *ababccb, abacbddc,* and *aaabcccb.* Counterpoint helps to make wholes from what without it might have been two parts. *Even-song,* for instance, rhymes *abbacddc,* a pattern obviously susceptible to a center split; its line lengths, however (35443445), by countering its rhyme plan, alleviate the strain at the middle. Herbert learned to give himself more working room, then, by composing firmly organized, sizable stanzas.

He also learned to make the technical aspects of his verse count for more in conveying meaning. Feminine endings, as he discovered, could, if consistently placed, qualify the contents of the lines in which they appeared. In *Sepulchre* (*a*5, *a*5, *a*5, *b*1, *c*5, *c*5, *c*5, *b*1), the *a*- and *c*-rhymes are all masculine, the *b*-rhymes all feminine. This particular distinction of the bob and wheel lines from the longer ones parallels their ideological difference from the main lines. The long ones describe Christ's body, postulate Him as living law, whereas the short, feminine ones indicate His treatment by mankind (*Receive thee, They leave thee, To hold thee,* etc.). The thesis-arsis line endings complement this contrast. Feminine endings complement grammatical mode in *Sighs and grones,* where the imperative beginnings and endings of the stanzas frame the poet's acknowledgment of his unworthiness:

> O do not blinde me!
> I have deserv'd that an Egyptian night
> Should thicken all my powers; because my lust
> Hath still sow'd fig-leaves to exclude thy light:
> But I am frailtie, and already dust;
> O do not grinde me! (83)

The two *b*-rhymes of *Dialogue* (*a*4, *b*3, *a*4, *b*3, *c*4, *c*4, *c*4, *c*4,) are feminine, and thereby the shift in tone and rhythm between the first and last halves of each stanza is heightened, the near-ballad form of the first half giving way to the more level, sustained verse of the last four lines. Each of the strophes of the hymn section of *An Offering* begins with two feminine lines, which resolve into the stronger end words of the conclusion. And with the greatest ingenuity, Herbert highlights the short lines of *Praise* (II) by giving them feminine endings, firmly separating them from the others and calling attention to the fact that the odd stanzas are "I-Thee" strophes, the even, "Thou-me" ones:

King of Glorie, King of Peace,
   I will love thee:
And that love may never cease,
   I will move thee.

Thou hast granted my request,
   Thou hast heard me:
Thou didst note my working breast,
   Thou hast spar'd me.

Wherefore with my utmost art
   I will sing thee,
And the cream of all my heart
   I will bring thee. (146)

In some cases, the feminine rhymes do duty primarily within the stanza, while in others—*Praise* (II), notably—they point up relationships between two or more separate groups of lines. In his late verse Herbert increasingly availed himself of other kinds of stanza linking. Five of the Williams MS. poems (*The Sacrifice, Grace, Praise* (I), *The Pearl,* and *Unkindnesse*) contain refrains, and this early one can mark Herbert's realization of the value of gradual alterations in a conspicuously-placed refrain. That of *The Pearl* is too familiar to require comment; that of *Praise* (I) follows Herbert's argument as he promises greater and greater dedication of his efforts, beginning with *Thou shalt have more* and concluding with *And much, much more;* that of *Unkindnesse* progresses steadily from *I would not use a friend, as I use Thee,* to *Yet use I not my foes, as I use Thee.* When one surveys the new poems in *The Temple,* he can but conclude that Herbert liked this device, for he used it thirteen times.[6] One might even say that *Aaron* consists entirely of refrain material, so closely do each of the five lines of each stanza follow their counterparts in the others, the first ones treating the symbolism of the priest's head, the second ones, that of the breast, the third ones, that of the bells, the fourth ones, that of the rest afforded by the bells, and the last ones, the total dressing of the servant of God. Most of the thirteen poems do not make such extreme use of repetition; they, like *Praise* (I) and *Unkindnesse,* contain refrains altered stanza by stanza in accommodation to the progression of the argument.

And just as Herbert attached more and more refrains to his stanzas in an effort to trace the course of their relationship, he initiated increasing numbers of stanzas within a single poem with similar first lines. Only nine early poems incorporate this comparative technique; seventeen of the late ones do.[7] Sometimes all of the strophes begin similarly, as is true in *Vertue, Mortification,* and *Constancie,* to name three; other times—in *The Banquet, Vanitie* (I), *Conscience,* and *Mattens*—a group of stanzas is separated from the others by their corresponding beginnings. All of the likenesses, however, point up significant relationships of idea among the units thus associated.

Linking of related stanzas through non-refrain rhyme repetition, and its accompanying delineation of argumentative structure, figures more prominently in the late poems than in the ones of the Williams MS., where only twice does one find it. The two stanzas of *Easter-wings* have their likeness emphasized not only by means of their bizarre common shape, but through word repetitions within the line and rhyme echoes in corresponding lines (*store, same, more, became, poore, thee, rise, harmoniously, victories, me* in the second). Another Williams MS. poem, *Ode,* retitled *Antiphon* (II) in *The Temple,* contains stanza linking designed to reinforce its content, the first three stanzas recording the antiphonal singing of men and angels, the last stanza the unifying of their song. Beginning with the second stanza, each stanza picks up its initial rhyme from the next-to-last line of the stanza preceding it.

Apparently Herbert saw many possibilities in such stanza linking, for among the last poems are a number containing permutations of it—*The Church-floore, The*

Quip, Businesse, Sinnes Round, Complaining, Clasping of hands, Praise (III), and *The Posie*. See, for example, the first section of *The Church-floore*:

> Mark you the floore? that square & speckled stone,
>   Which looks so firm and strong,
>   Is *Patience:*
>
> And th' other black and grave, wherewith each one
>   Is checker'd all along,
>   *Humilitie:*
>
> The gentle rising, which on either hand
>   Leads to the Quire above,
>   **Is** *Confidence:*
>
> But the sweet cement, which in one sure band
>   Ties the whole frame is *Love*
>   And *Charitie.* (66-67)

This rhyme plan, charting as it does the subtle relationship of the four groups of lines, represents a marked development of Herbert's technique over that of even such a neat structure as *Antiphon* (II). In one sense, each of the four stanzas is parallel with the others since it names an allegorical equivalent for a part of the church floor. The first two, however, have a special kinship, as they point out kinds of stones; appropriately, then, they are bound together by the *stone-one* and *strong-along* rhymes. The same is true of stanzas three and four: they call attention to parts of the floor besides the stones, and so their *hand-band* and *above-love* link is fitting. The *Patience-Humilitie-Confidence-Charitie* sequence of the four concluding lines, however, in addition to suggesting the checkered pattern of the squares, provides a contrapuntal effect to what otherwise might have become a too-pat rhyme arrangement. Although the first two lines of each stanza give an *aabb* arrangement to the whole poem, the last lines do not sustain this relationship, but, considered separately, impart an *abab* form to the stanzas. Thus, Herbert avoids the monotony which might well have resulted from a completely consistent rhyme plan among such short lines.

Businesse, another new poem, makes comparably elaborate use of rhyme echoes. Each of the significant meaning units treats a different topic; lines 1-14 (rhyming *play, day, one, gone, none, tears, fears, forbears, plot, hot, not, grones, bones, ones*) deal with the officious soul in relationship to its proud self; lines 15-28 (rhyming *be, thee, throne, bone, none, thee, wretchedly, fee, plot, forgot, not, thee, miserie, be*), the soul in relationship to the Incarnation; lines 29-38 (rhyming *breath, death, drosse, crosse, losse, vein, again, gain, kneels, feels*), the soul's sensitivity to both good and evil. After the introductory couplet, the first section is framed by the rhymes *one-gone-none* and *grones-bones-ones.* A similar, though not identical, repetition marks off the second section *(be-thee, thee-miserie-be).* And the two sections are forced into particularly close parallel by their similar rhymes *one-gone-none* and *throne-bone-none* in the first tercets, *plot-hot-not* and *plot-forgot-not* in the third. The concluding section, a resolution of the disparate first passages, contains no rhyme echoes. Rather Herbert substitutes strong syntactical parallels between the two tercets within the section:

> He that loseth gold, though drosse,
> Tells to all he meets his crosse:
> He that sinnes, hath he no losse?
>
> He that findes a silver vein,
> Thinks on it, and thinks again:
> Brings thy Saviours death no gain? (114)

The whole arrangement is managed with much cleverness. The first two sections, seemingly such opposites, are forced into forms so similar that surely every reader must notice the likeness. Then comes the concluding synthesis, the belief that the unfeeling person is incapable of being touched either by great sin or great goodiness: "Who in heart not ever kneels, / Neither sinne nor Saviour feels." (114) This couplet can be emotionally realized by the reader only after he recognizes Herbert's formal paralleling of the two members of the sin-virtue dichotomy.

The other late poems embodying stanza linking may be mentioned briefly. In *Praise* (III) Herbert ends each stanza with *more,* suggesting the spinning of praise promised at the opening of the poem; *Sinnes round,* already mentioned, has its circularity limned by rhyme repetitions, as does *Clasping of hands;* the four stanzas of *Complaining* are divided into two groups by the rhymes linking the first two and last two stanzas *(aabb calls, ccdd falls, eeff grief, gghh relief),* a separation corresponding to the logical structure of the piece; and in *Dotage,* a catalogue of human "False glozing pleasures," Herbert dramatizes the common vainglory of mankind by ending each stanza of the poem with the same rhyme—*career-here* in the first, *clear-here* in the second, and *cleare-here* in the third. Rhyme echoes, then, as well as varied refrains and similar beginnings of stanzas, became a part of Herbert's repertory of devices for expressing meaning.

Perhaps the most interesting of such devices is the variation of rhyme patterning. Quite early, Herbert decided to discard variation as an end in itself. One of the six Williams MS. poems which he omitted from the final version of *The Temple* is *Trinity Sunday,* his closest approach to free verse *(a2, a1, b2, b2, c2, c4, d3, d2, d3, e4, f2, f4, g2, g3, a3, h2, e5, a2, h1).* Evidently he disapproved of the experiment, since he discarded the verse and thereafter used variation solely as a sort of poetic shorthand for disorder or laxness. Three other poems in the early group deviate from strict stanzaic regularity, but they do so in a quite different way. *Deniall* and *Antiphon* (II), both mentioned above, contain rhyme irregularities which express spiritual dryness and separateness, respectively. *Man,* also

in the Williams collection, has a flexible design of great
ingenuity.[8] Its rhyme scheme is different in nearly every
stanza, though the line lengths remain constant throughout
(354453). Four features of the patterning are significant:
the plan which Herbert uses most frequently in six-line
stanzas, and which apparently represents the norm for him,
ababcc, does not occur until the last stanza; stanzas two and
eight follow the same scheme, *abcabc;* stanzas two through
five imitate the scheme of their predecessors but for one
line displacement; stanzas six through nine undergo more
extensive changes.[9] The poem is, then, divided into two
parts by means of the degree of rhyme inversion from
previous stanzas—the first part, one through five, the second,
six through nine. These mechanical arrangements reinforce
the logical structure of the poem. It begins with Biblical
commonplace:

> My God, I heard this day,
> That none doth build a stately habitation,
> But he that means to dwell therein.
> What house more stately hath there been,
> Or can be, than is Man? to whose creation
> All things are in decay. (90)

The three stanzas following give a largely impersonal
commentary on the eminence of man. In the fifth, however,
one notices a marked change to a more personal realization
of the ministry of the universe to man: "For us the windes
do blow, / The earth doth rest, heav'n move, and fountains
flow." (91) This intimate vein continues until the last
stanza but one, when Herbert prepares for his conclusion
by returning to a discussion of man in general, reproaching
him for his indifference to the services of the universe. In
the last stanza all of the various strands are knit up: man
at large is reminded of his proper place in the order of
things, a place between God and the world; the poet and

general man are treated as one, the personal dominating as Herbert prays for God to dwell in the house of man's body:

> Since then, my God, thou hast
> So brave a Palace built; O Dwell in it,
>   That it may dwell with thee at last!
>   Till then, afford us so much wit;
> That, as the world serves us, we may serve thee,
>   And both thy servants be. (92)

He has come back to the metaphor of the beginning, and to some of its diction *(my God, built, dwell),* changing it from a general statement that is secondhand knowledge to a general-personal one that he has realized in the course of the poem. The familiar rhyme scheme of the last stanza is most suitable for such a confident affirmation; the changing stanza forms are clearly appropriate to his exploratory mood; the link of the beginning and the end is no mere mechanical device; and the difference in the degree of change occurring in stanza patterns coincides with the thematic shifts at stanza five.

Seven poems in the final version of *The Temple* change stanza design halfway through—the most conspicuous and emphatic means of making rhyme dramatize a significant change in tone or situation. In addition, five new poems show some kind of formal variation. The final unrhymed line of *Grief,* much like those of the first stanzas of *Deniall,* expresses discord and lack of harmony with God; *Businesse,* discussed above, consists of three sections, the first two different in theme but formally identical, and the last, a synthesis of the abbreviated and compressed. In *Love unknown,* Herbert chronicles previous efforts to reach and please God, following, as the standard verse, an *abab* pentameter design. Three times in the course of the poem, however, he injects a note of intensified dissonance by abbreviating lines to dimeters—all fitful little exclamations:

But when I thought to sleep out all these faults
                              (I sigh to speak)
I found that some had stuff'd the bed with thoughts,
I would say *thorns.* Deare, could my heart not break. . . .
                              (130)

In the last strophe of *Home,* Herbert wrenches rhyme to
prove the distortion of his verse, as well as the languishing
of his soul, in God's absence:

> Come dearest Lord, passe not this holy season,
>   My flesh and bones and joynts do pray:
> And ev'n my verse, when by the ryme and reason
>   The word is, *Stay,* sayes ever, *Come.* (109)

The Temple's most famous dramatization of rebellion
and disorder, *The Collar,* presents problems of some complexity. In his commentary on its structure, Joseph Summers comes very close to what I feel is the true principle
of its arrangement:

Although readers accustomed to Renaissance poetry might
feel uncomfortable with the disorder of the first thirty-two
lines, they could hardly divine the stanzaic norm which is
the measure for that disorder until it is established simultaneously with the submission of the rebel in the final quatrain: $10^a4^b8^a6^b$. That pattern of line lengths and rhyme
does not occur until the final four lines; with those lines
the elements of the pattern are arranged so as to form almost the mathematical ultimate in lack of periodicity. If
we consider that the first thirty-two lines represent eight
quatrains, we discover six different patterns of rhyme and
seven patterns of line lengths.[10]

It is true, surely, that the final quatrain is a resolution of
disorder, but the resolution is a commutation of a pattern
faintly discernible in the first thirty-two lines but artfully
obscured by some inversions of rhymes, some intrusive
rhymes, and tensions between line divisions and semantic

groups. There are six natural rhyme groups before the final cross rhyme pattern: *abcba, deadce, fgfhh, dijdji, gkkg,* and *lbmmlb.* The first is, except for the intruding *c*-rhyme, an enclosed rhyme quatrain. The second, *deadce,* has a certain degree of balance because of the two *d*'s and *e*'s, but this balance is blurred by the substitution of *ce* and *ea* in the last two lines. The third rhyme group, *fgfhh,* has similar balance and similar deviation. The fourth, *dijdji,* shows the interlocked structure and the parallelism of the *abab* design, with some disturbance of the balance by the change of *ij* to *ji.* The fifth rhyme group is something like the first except that it is a true *abba* type with no added elements. And the last group before the conclusion, *lbmmlb,* actually crowds the edges of the *abab* form, being distinguished by the couplet in the middle. The first thirty-two lines, then, are not completely formless; they are, rather, distorted versions of the tranquil measure of the conclusion. While varied, however, the groups are not randomly arranged. The first five lines and lines 27-32, similar in rhyme scheme, are also parallel in diction:

> I struck the board, and cry'd, No more.
> I will abroad.
> What? shall I ever sigh and pine?
> My lines and life are free; free as the rode,
> Loose as the winde, as large as store.
>
> .   .   .   .   .
>
> Away; take heed:
> I will abroad.
> Call in thy deaths head there: tie up thy fears. (153)

Not only the rhyme plans, but the rhythms and short word groups of these two passages are similar. The rhymes, then, reinforce the structure within the first thirty-two lines as well as divide this section from the final quatrain. For the mature Herbert, disorder was not attractive; and so he here only feigns a confusion that is actually well controlled.

This formal irregularity, unlike that of the discarded *Trinity Sunday,* is a dramatic device, one of the poem's chief instruments of utterance.

TO APPRECIATE the numerous aspects of Herbert's development is not to disavow the excellence of the early poems in *The Temple.* Pieces like *The Pearl,* the Jordan poems, and *The Sacrifice* need no apology. They, however, like the shaped poems, are quite specialized types of sacred verse, and one admires them for their uniqueness as well as for their intrinsic worth. One happy result of Herbert's growth as a poet is that he envisioned and executed so many new modes of devotional expression that he did not depreciate the value of his early verses by proliferation. In the total context of *The Temple* they gain, rather, by the diversity with which they are surrounded. The "fine variety" that Herbert conceded to foreign languages graces his own work, a variety brought about largely by the addition of the late poems. And in the late poems, one also finds him adding to the store of techniques which distinguish the germinal section of *The Temple.* Close control and more subtle use of imagery, firmer integration of stanzas, and the enlisting of prosodical devices as aids to thematic expression—characteristics of his final achievement—prove that even this superb poet found ways to improve his art.

5

The Clothing of the Sonne: Complexity in Apparent Simplicity

SHERLOCK HOLMES might well have been speaking of *The Temple* when, chatting with Watson about the Boscombe Valley adventure, he commented that it was one of those simple cases which are so extremely difficult. Surface tidiness and an aura of the commonplace are likely to prevent many kinds of close inspection, whether the object at hand is a problem in ratiocination or a collection of poems which read as easily as Herbert's do. Despite the range and quantity of materials which modern scholarship has revealed in *The Temple,* many readers still approach it armed with formulae gleaned from anthology headnotes, and skim and sample instead of giving the full consideration which such superb verse deserves. Treated thus, it yields little besides an impression of facile utterance of devout orthodoxy. To some extent, probably, many readers have always undervalued *The Temple*. It has been Herbert's dubious fortune that popular estimation of his poetic gifts has been shaped by a misunderstanding of his admirers' tributes to his serenity and humility. Among his immediate followers he was known as holy Mr. Herbert, and this label, rather than the accomplishments of his art, influenced many of his imitators; in the eighteenth century he was best known in the fifty-two Wesley adulterations, but was also recommended as wholesome reading for young people;[1] in the nineteenth century his conceits were usually adjudged regrettably eccentric but were overlooked in deference to his piety. Critics of our own time routinely praise him as the master of homely metaphor, or as the supremely Anglican metaphysical poet. In a memorable comparison, Mr. Eliot has commented that in Donne thought seems in control of feeling, but that in Herbert feeling seems in control of thought.[2] Now, all of these observations are as true as they are complimentary. Surely no one would gainsay Herbert's holiness, the unlikelihood of his tarnishing readers of any age, or his extraordinarily felicitous choice of materials from the everyday world. Yet the frequently epigrammatic characterizations of these virtues, made in the best of faith, have led countless readers to regard Herbert's verse as worthwhile because of its author's holiness, or as fit solely for the unsophisticated, or as the vessel of only the homeliest of imagery. Any one of these misconceptions is certain to diminish one's respect for *The Temple;* several of them together almost inevitably produce the impression of a body of writing at once sweet, sectarian, and altogether ingenuous—an impression which keeps many people from reading Herbert with enough care to discover his intellectual toughness and his richness of allusion.

Improper consideration of certain qualities of the verse has nurtured the image of Herbert as a sweetish singer. Chief among these are the smoothness of his lyrics' surfaces and the obvious orderliness of their structures. How curious that a poet's technical genius should be turned into evidence of narrowness of sensibility! In Herbert's case, however, it has been done. The various modern defenses of Donne's irregular rhythms on the grounds of their masculinity, of their being decorous reflections of the complexity of his thought, or of their being necessitated by the tortuous nature of the experience being related, have left many readers feeling that a Herbert, writing in perfect rhythms and melodious lines, can have little to say that is subtle or even out of the ordinary. Herbert is made to play Surrey to Donne's Wyatt, since, obviously, a man who doesn't allow his iambs to get out of hand is incapable of a really personal poetic statement.

Companionate nonsense has been made of his highly-finished stanza patterns. Many contemporary readers are touched by the childlike piety of mind that would lead a man to make a poem about an altar or about wings look like its subject, not realizing that he was suiting a Greek convention to Christian worship, or that would prompt his efforts to devise such an unprecedented number of stanza forms. Were Palmer's remarks about the stanzaic variety (another encomium kindly intentioned but sometimes ill used) not repeated as often as they are, I doubt that most readers would think of it as one of Herbert's cardinal principles, so surely and unobtrusively is each pattern adapted to the poem in which it figures (recall, for example, the spare and restrained stanza of *Discipline,* the prosodic bombast of *The Collar,* the stately but enjambed strophes of *Church-monuments,* eminently appropriate for a poem about death and physical dissolution); and as wisely selected are many of the traditional forms for their function in *The Temple* (the sonnet for *Love* (I) and *Love* (II), a standard didactic stanza for *The Church-porch,* a standard *aubade* stanza for *The Dawning,* and so on).

Herbert's structures are usually tidy, to many readers a characteristic possible in lyrics only in combination with simplicity. One of his favorite structural devices is a series of conspicuously parallel stanzas. Needless to say, poems arranged in such a manner frequently are flawed either by stiffness or by gratuitous repetition. In most such poems in *The Temple,* however, the parallels function as unstated central metaphors, suggesting likenesses between quantities not commonly associated. In *The Pearl,* for example, learning, honor, and pleasure are shown to be equally useful, but only inasmuch as they teach one the value of the pearl of the kingdom of Heaven; in *Vanitie* (I) an astronomer, a diver, and an alchemist are typified as similarly earthbound, destructive, and sensual; the nearly duplicate stanzas of *Easter-wings* cleverly involve Herbert with all mankind in the benefits of the Fortunate Fall, the first unit setting forth the decay and regeneration of man as a species, the second, that of Herbert in particular; the first three stanzas of *Vertue* prove all of the beauties of the natural world inferior to that of the virtuous soul; the two stanzas of *Clasping of hands* demonstrate the basic pattern of Christian experience—with Herbert becoming God's, then God becoming Herbert's. These poems containing noticeably paralleled stanzas, as well as many others which could be described, join consummate neatness with consummate delicacy of perception. The simplicity of their appearance does not accompany simplification of idea.

All of these characteristics of formal neatness spring from two sources, I believe. First, Herbert was assuredly a man who yearned towards order and regularity of all kinds, from the efficient running of his household to tranquility of soul. Most naturally, then, his verse reveals the mind of its maker. Yet a second and more specific impetus affects the highly stylized format of *The Temple*: the volume is, as Herbert explains in *The Dedication,* his offering to God, his first fruits, in reality only a return of God's gifts to him. And for Herbert, as one finds again and again in *The Temple,* God's gift to man was the whole created universe, an ever awesome miracle of seasonal balance and cosmic harmony, seen in the perspective of time as comprehensible and perfectly designed history. The return of such a gift would, to a man like Herbert, necessitate outward as well as inward order.

The surface smoothness and meticulous organization of Herbert's verse should not be confused with any of the several kinds of genuine simplicity and limitation to be found in Renaissance verse, or with the *naif* posing affected by some Elizabethan poetic lovers when they attempted to discard Petrarchanism. Traherne, for example, by the very selection of the perspective of infant-eye forced a sharp restriction of theme, subject, imagery, and mood, thereby excluding much of the richness to be found in all of his prose and in the *Serious and Pathetical Contemplation of the Mercies of God;* Southwell, one feels, imposed a similar selectivity on much of his poetry when he chose to make it the sacred counterpart of popular romantic song. The verse of Crashaw, although sensuously gorgeous, only occasionally departs from quite modest venues of imagery and tone: it shows its maker's uncomplicated, though for his nationality unusual, concept of devotion. And one has only to move to the very minor poets of the period—such imitators of Herbert as John Collop, Ralph Knevnet, or Rowland Watkyns—to witness true limitation of invention and imagery.

The range of Herbert's figurative language is large, much larger than is commonly believed. And in kind, it is not unlike Donne's, different though the poetries of the two men obviously are. If one looks through *The Temple* for the kinds of tropes frequently cited as most typical of Donne, he will find most of them. Herbert relies as heavily as Donne on legal metaphor; it appears as a minor motif in dozens of his poems, and constitutes one of the important figures of *The Reprisall, Redemption, Sepulchre, Affliction* (II), *To all Angels and Saints, Lent, Submission, Justice* (I), *Obedience, The Size, The Holdfast, The Discharge,*

Dooms-day, and *Judgment*. He, also, likes the imagery of mercantilism (sometimes blending with that of the law), making it appear prominently in *The Sinner, Love* (II), *Praise* (I), *Affliction* (II), *Even-song, Constancie, Affliction* (III), *Sunday, Avarice, Employment* (III), *Ungratefulnesse, The Pearl, Prayer* (II), *Obedience, Vanitie* (II), *Dialogue, Giddinesse, The Discharge, An Offering, Clasping of hands,* and *The Odour*. He makes as full use of military comparison as Donne does in his devotional verse: one finds it at the center of the argument in *The Thanksgiving, The Reprisall, Nature, Affliction* (I), *The H. Communion, Frailtie, Deniall, Affliction* (IV), *Antiphon* (II), *Artillerie,* and *Discipline*. He is interested in astronomy, alchemy, archery, the use of firearms, cardplaying, falconry, wrestling and fencing, running and vaulting, bowling, affairs of the court, in the stamped faces on coins, in medicine, in mining and metallurgy, in navigation, in clothing and dressing, in cosmetics, in animals and insects, in the curious properties of windows and mirrors, in dreams. And so one could continue. Most of the kinds of "Donnean" imagery are amply represented in Herbert's verse.

Herbert has, of course, favorite categories of imagery quite different from those generally associated with Donne. It is far from my intention to claim the figurative repertories of the two men to be near-duplicates. I merely hope to exorcise the notion that the verse of *The Temple* differs from Donne's devotional poetry in large measure because of a markedly divergent selection of metaphor, and above all, to dispel the belief that they differ because of Herbert's reliance on scanter and more commonplace tropological materials. One must, I am convinced, look elsewhere to discover grounds which will account for Donne's verse sounding like Donne and Herbert's like himself.

Chief among such grounds, surely, is Herbert's manner of subordinating to the skeleton of his overtly stated argument the very images which Donne uses for startlingly dramatic effect, with the result that many tissues of metaphor in *The Temple* go unnoticed. When Donne likens some aspect of love to an astronomical phenomenon, for example, much of the piquance of the comparison rests on the obvious technicality of his language. At the conclusion of *A Valediction: of the Booke,* he promises that his forthcoming journey will only serve to increase his appreciation of the lady:

> How great love is, presence best tryall makes,
> But absence tryes how long this love will bee:
> To take a latitude
> Sunne or starres, are fitliest view'd
> At their brightest, but to conclude
> Of longitudes, what other way have wee,
> But to marke when, and where the darke eclipses bee?

Or in *Loves Growth:*

> If, as in water stir'd more circles bee
> Produc'd by one, love such additions take,
> Those like so many spheares, but one heaven make,
> For, they are all concentrique unto thee.

The explicitness of the empirical matters described lends credence to his avowal of love: the lover is successful because his scientific argot temporarily distracts the lady and forestalls her incipient objection to the quite tenuous parallel between the arrangement of the heavens and the nature of love. Donne's scientific correlatives, unassailable as science, are so conspicuously correct, that his forced analogies seem acceptable indeed.

Contrast these with one or two of Herbert's allusions to celestial bodies. The first two stanzas of *The Glance* are devoted to an account of the pleasure occasioned by the poet's first awareness of God's regard. In the final strophe, he speculates on the joy of seeing Him face to face after death:

If thy first glance so powerful be,
A mirth but open'd and seal'd up again;
What wonders shall we feel, when we shall see
Thy full-ey'd love!
When thou shalt look us out of pain,
And one aspect of thine spend in delight
More then a thousand sunnes disburse in light,
In heav'n above. (172)

To dramatize the shift from seeing God on earth to seeing
Him in Heaven, Herbert introduces the system of astronomical imagery which gives full point to the title of the
poem. Now, there is every bit as much technical language
here as in either of the two Donne specimens quoted above.
Glance means a sudden movement producing a flash of
light, or the flash or gleam itself; *full,* of course, refers to a
familiar planetary phase; *aspect,* to the relative positions
of heavenly bodies as they appear to a person on the earth
at a given time; *disburse,* to open or scatter out rays of
light. Yet the stanza is not as overwhelmingly "scientific"
as are the Donne analogues, largely because each of the
technical terms has a strong non-technical connotation.
One's first impression upon reading the lines is of the
emotional intensity with which the speaker anticipates the
full glance; only secondarily does one realize Herbert's
intimation through the language of astronomy that God's
light outshines all human perception of the material
heavens. The poet appears deliberately to have subordi-
nated the rational workings of the figurative language to
emotional impact. Mr. Eliot is right: here feeling seems in
control of thought.

Something of the same effect is achieved in the first
stanza of *Vanitie* (I), where the astronomical terms double
to convey general meanings as well:

The fleet Astronomer can bore,
And thred the spheres with his quick-piercing minde:

> He views their stations, walks from doore to doore,
>   Surveys, as if he had design'd
> To make a purchase there: he sees their dances,
>   And knoweth long before
> Both their full-ey'd aspects, and secret glances. (85)

A professional vocabulary is here: in this passage, also, one finds *aspects* and *glances*: a *station* is the apparent standing still of a planet at its apogee and perigee; a *dance* is the apparent flicker of a star; a *purchase,* the exertion of mechanical power or leverage; *spheres* and *surveys* are, of course, immediately understandable. Yet the somewhat smug familiarity of the astronomer with his subject is, I believe, what Herbert intends us to notice first about this stanza, and so the technical words are chosen to suggest an almost human-to-human relationship between starman and planets. The consciousness of the reader is not assaulted, as it frequently is in Donne, by unequivocally scientific terminology.

This principle could be illustrated by almost every poem in *The Temple;* let it suffice to view a handful more. Herbert is fond of the metaphor of ocean travel. In the first stanza of *The Bunch of Grapes,* he uses it to heighten the general idea of regression:

> Joy, I did lock thee up: but some bad man
>   Hath let thee out again:
> And now, me thinks, I am where I began
>   Sev'n yeares ago: one vogue and vein,
>   One aire of thoughts usurps my brain.
> I did toward Canaan draw; but now I am
> Brought back to the Red sea, the sea of shame. (128)[3]

Lock had the same nautical significance in Herbert's day that it does now; *vogue* meant the course of a vessel; *vein* denoted either a wind or a current of water; the *aire of thoughts* caused a ship to change its course. Herbert has, then, chosen the figure of the voyage of sensibility, a fixture

of English verse since the early Middle Ages, to accompany
his symbolic backward movement to the sea of shame, and
most appropriately, since water figures so prominently in
the Biblical account of the journey. It is, however, the
Biblical parallels of the stanza—the seven years, the Red
Sea, Canaan—which probably attract the first attention of
most readers; the vocabulary of navigation, much like that
of astronomy in *The Glance* and *Vanitie* (I), is so thoroughly blended with the other threads of the fabric that
it is easy to overlook.

Easy, also, to overlook is the additional dimension
provided many poems in *The Temple* by the metaphors of
sports, for Herbert rarely names the game. At the beginning of *The Method,* he typifies God as a bowler, aiming at
man but hindered by a *rub,* an irregularity in the green:

> Poore heart, lament.
> For since thy God refuseth still,
> There is some rub, some discontent,
> Which cools his will. (133)

In *Affliction* (I), the speaker is the bowl itself, impelled
toward God, but diverted from its correct path:

> Turning my purge to food, thou throwest me
>   Into more sicknesses.
> Thus doth thy power crosse-bias me, not making
> Thine own gift good, yet me from my wayes taking. (48)

God appears in *Providence* as a master chess player, ordering the world according to the pattern of the game of
royalty:

> . . . Thou hast made poore sand
> Check the proud sea, ev'n when it swells and gathers.
>   .   .   .   .   .
> How finely dost thou times and seasons spin,
> And make a twist checker'd with night and day! (118)

Herbert wrestles with God in the first stanza of *Nature*:

> Full of rebellion, I would die,
> Or fight, or travell, or denie
> That thou hast ought to do with me.
> O tame my heart;
> It is thy highest art
> To captivate strong holds to thee. (45)

In *H. Baptisme* (II), God is shown to overpower man early: "On my infancie / Thou didst lay hold, and antedate / My faith in me." (44) Herbert, like Donne, was fascinated by humanly determined symbols of value—jewels, coins, clothes—and he used them both to show the slight worth of much earthly traffic and, conversely, to familiarize his statements about spiritual matters. And, as is true of the metaphors mentioned above, these symbols are usually intimated, not directly named or described. Herbert found the coin, for example, a useful symbol for man's being made in the image of God, precious because of this resemblance, not through any intrinsic merit. Yet most frequently, the coin functions without being named. In *The Church-porch,* Herbert tries to show the debasement of drunkenness: "Be not a beast in courtesie; but stay, / Stay at the third cup, or forgo the place, / Wine above all things doth Gods stamp deface." (8) Wine causes man to revert to the bestial part of his double nature, and, by implication, to lose the celestial; it also causes him to blur God's image stamped in him, and so to devalue himself. A more elaborate, yet still unstated, man-as-coin figure runs throughout *The Sinner*:

> Lord, how I am all ague, when I seek
> What I have treasur'd in my memorie!
> Since, if my soul make even with the week,
> Each seventh note by right is due to thee.
> I finde there quarries of pil'd vanities,
> But shreds of holinesse, that dare not venture

To show their face, since crosse to thy decrees:
There the circumference earth is, heav'n the centre.
In so much dregs the quintessence is small:
  The spirit and good extract of my heart
  Comes to about the many hundred part.
Yet Lord restore thine image, heare my call:
  And though my hard heart scarce to thee can grone,
  Remember that thou once didst write in stone. (38)

Here the speaker conceives himself as a coin faced with God's image only when he has been a participant in good deeds. But the coins in his treasury, the quintessence or gold, exist in such pitifully small proportion to the dregs, or quarried ore, that they are ashamed to show their faces; and though the protagonist's heart is as hard as the rock from which the gold is extracted, he is confident that God, who once proved to Moses that He could engrave stone, will re-impress Himself on even the basest contents of his soul. The whole man will then become coin of the heavenly Realm. One has only to contrast this treatment of the figure with that of *A Valediction: of Weeping* to realize the extent of Herbert's understatement: "For thy face coines them, and thy stampe they beare, / And by this Mintage they are something worth. . . ." Donne labels his coins; Herbert, here and elsewhere, does not.

Many people assume a simplicity in Herbert's verse because, unlike some metaphysical poets, he usually makes a clear statement of the general themes of his poems. Almost any reader can grasp what almost any Herbert poem is "about," since rarely are subject and argument presented solely in the implications of the figurative language. Thus one can read *The Sacrifice* and get a strong impression of the bitter irony of the all-compassionate Christ's treatment by the Jews, even though he may never have heard of religious typology; *Redemption*'s involved parable of leases, possessions, and suits is explained by its title; both the imagery and argument of *Repentance* are involved and difficult, but its aphoristic last line ("Fractures well cur'd make us more strong") enlightens both—to mention three poems with different kinds of informative devices, which, outside of the major imageries, insure the reader's recognition of their purposes. Critics differ vigorously among themselves over interpretative details of *The Collar* and *Jordan* (I) and *Jordan* (II), but any reader approaching these poems for the first time perceives that in the first, the speaker is rebelling against religious discipline, and in the pair of poems about poetry, Herbert is arraigning some kind of glib poetic artifice.

Such partial recognition has led many to think of Herbert's verse as less complex than that of Donne, in which, quite frequently, one's understanding of a poetic statement is entirely dependent upon his appreciating the implications of the imagery. Unless, for example, one remembers the relationship of influences and spheres, and unless he is familiar with the medieval formula for angels' becoming visible to the human eye, he can make little or nothing of *Aire and Angels;* and unless he happens to know of the Fathers' gloss of the incident of Christ among the doctors as symbolic of His whole ministry, he will be puzzled to account for the appropriateness of the fourth of the *Holy Sonnets* dedicated to Lady Magdalene Herbert;[4] unless he pays close attention indeed to the arbitrary-value symbols of *A Valediction: of Weeping,* he will miss the poem's dramatic situation and its total commentary on separation; without the most devoted delectation of the imagery and allusions of *Good Friday. Riding Westward,* he will be likely to make nothing at all of that splendid meditation. Small wonder that, humbled by the quite awesome magnitude of fact and inference requisite to arriving at even the most rudimentary ideas of much of Donne's verse, the reader is impressed with its complexity.

Many Herbert poems of similar complexity pass frequently as luminous but rather easy devotions. In *The H.*

Scriptures (I), for example, Herbert praised the Bible as sweet and healing, and for many readers, the sonnet does not transcend these commonplaces.

> Oh Book, infinite sweetnesse! let my heart
>   Suck ev'ry letter, and a hony gain,
>   Precious for any grief in any part;
> To cleare the breast, to mollifie all pain.
> Thou art all health, health thriving till it make
>   A full eternitie: thou art a masse
>   Of strange delights, where we may wish & take.
> Ladies, look here; this is the thankfull glasse,
> That mends the lookers eyes: this is the well
>   That washes what it shows. Who can indeare
>   Thy praise too much? thou art heav'ns Lidger here,
> Working against the states of death and hell.
>   Thou art joyes handsell: heav'n lies flat in thee,
>   Subject to ev'ry mounters bended knee. (58)

A close consideration of the imagery reveals an eminently explicit statement about the scriptures: it is a book which heals and delights because it reveals the nature of heaven in terms of human beings and the activities of the Church. Herbert's choice of honey to typify the sweetness of God's word is far from careless. Honey is, first, a standard Biblical symbol, occurring in two famous passages in the Psalms: "How sweet are thy words unto my taste! yea, sweeter than honey to my mouth!" (119:103); "More to be desired are they than gold, yea, than much fine gold: sweeter also than honey and the honeycomb. Moreover by them is thy servant warned: and in keeping of them there is great reward" (19:10-11). Patristic tradition adds significantly to what Scriptural text says about honey and honeycombs. St. Ambrose and Bernard of Clairvaux figured the Church as a beehive, the perfectly organized community, producing sweetness and eloquence.[5] By the time of Dante, swarming bees had come to be associated with heaven. At the beginning of the thirty-first canto of the *Paradiso,* Dante sees the

ranks of the redeemed as the petals of a white rose, while
bee-like angels, inverting the practice of actual bees, swarm
around depositing honey from the presence of God. Herbert was patently fond of this association. In *The Starre,*
he uses it when anticipating his arrival in Heaven:

> Sure thou wilt joy, by gaining me
> To flie home like a laden bee
> Unto that hive of beams
> And garland-streams. (74)

In *Home,* he speaks of Christ leaving Heaven to assume
flesh: "There lay thy sonne: and must he leave that nest, /
That hive of sweetnesse. . . .?" (107) Apparently, then, in
The H. Scriptures (I), he intends the *infinite sweetnesse* of
scriptural honey to suggest the delights of Heaven, as well
as God's laws revealed to man.

 Honey, furthermore, was commonly employed as a
physic during Herbert's time. The Scriptures, in addition
to giving pleasure, heal, and heal in such a way that they
suggest the perfect well-being of Heaven, for they assuage
all pain, throughout a *full eternitie*—surely a deliberate
recall of the promise of the Apocalypse (21:4) that there
shall be no more death, sorrow, crying, nor pain, since
former things are passed away.

 Herbert moves on to two images neatly complementing
the honey-scriptures as purifying symbol of Church and
Heaven. They are a glass and a well. Both, of course,
reflect: the reader of the Testaments glimpses something
of himself in the accounts of personages of the Church.
At the same time, however, he is enabled to see more
clearly, and he is cleansed by the recognition. Both
processes are explicitly Biblical characterizations of the
larger life of Heaven; one of St. Paul's most widely-quoted
pronouncements concerns seeing in a glass darkly, but in
Heaven face to face; he also speaks of the transformation
effected in the gazer: "But we all, with open face beholding

as in a glass the glory of the Lord, are changed into the same image from glory to glory . . ." (II Cor. 3:18). The mirror of the Scriptures mends the vision of the beholder. As a well, it washes the person looking into it; and surely Herbert intended the careful reader to recall the Canticles' description of the Church as both honied of lips and a well of living waters (4:11, 15), and of Christ's assurance to the woman of Samaria that the water which He gave her was from a well springing up into eternal life (John 4:14).

The poem ends with a vigorous figure of the Bible as Heaven's ambassador, working, presumably through the Church, against the states (certainly a pun) of death and hell. Reverent address of this Lidger enables everyone to arrive at Heaven, a directly stated variation of the implications of earlier imagery. This poem, then, is no transparent paean; rather it is a careful and subtle statement of the Bible's position as mediator between man and deity. It is not really simple at all.

There is, however, one kind of actual simplicity in *The Temple,* that of language. Coleridge, commenting in the nineteenth chapter of the *Biographia* on *Love unknown,* points out that it conveys "the most fantastic thoughts in the most correct and natural language." While Coleridge censures Herbert on grounds that most twentieth-century readers cannot accept—we now know that the ideas of *Love unknown* are by no means as eccentric and novel as STC surmised[6]—he proves his awareness of a critical problem in Herbert which concerns every reader, that of the surprising combination of downright words and sophisticated conceptions. A part of the effect of linguistic easiness imparted by the verse arises from Herbert's preference for technical words which also carry a more general import. Another part, certainly, can be traced to his avoidance of proper names which might distract the reader from the devotional issue at hand, as we have seen in his remarkable skirting of the actual titles of classical deities. He seems purposely to omit other proper nouns as well. Except in *The Church Militant,* where the historical nature of the poem necessitates inclusion by name of many people and places, such nominations occur rarely. Many times Herbert seems at pains to circumvent exact names. At the beginning of *The Sonne,* for example, he defends his vernacular without mentioning any one language: "Let forrain nations of their language boast, / What fine varietie each tongue affords: / I like our language, as our men and coast. . . ." (167) He never singles out particular stars or constellations; his many references to voyages of discovery consistently eschew exact destinations; the only people directly identified are Bible characters; his numerous uses of exotic importations never give the origin of the product (contrast this situation with Donne's almost perfunctory mention of India when he refers to spices); his attention to history never evokes the name of any nation but those of the Jews and Egyptians, and they, like the people which he names, are Biblical.

Whenever a genus will serve his purpose as well as a species, he prefers the former. Among his dozens of references to flowers, only two are particularized—the rose and the lily (and this only once); he never distinguishes any of the orders of angels; though he is fond of alluding to precious stones, only twice does he name a particular jewel—the diamond in *Confession* and the pearl in *Vanitie* (I); poisons, medicines, and cordials, while figuring prominently in *The Temple,* remain general quantities; birds and beasts more often than not are undifferentiated; of the scores of references to sin, only pride and lust are specified, and only a handful of times; only a few of the most familiar theological terms appear *(Trinity, Incarnation, Salvation);* the large majority of instances of the imagery of clothes and dressing mention no specific garment; though *The Temple* abounds in suggestions of color, few hues are even mentioned.

An estimable part of one's impression of the simplicity

of the language of *The Temple* can be assigned, I believe, to this controlled generality of reference. It should not be confused with vagueness. In many instances, as I have already suggested, an apparently general word functions as the common purveyance of two sharply defined systems of metaphor and so is the most accurate possible term. Elsewhere the general wording of the imagery stands in evident subordination to a direct statement of theme, so that any reader can apprehend the principal subject, but so that the attentive reader, he who sees that "this verse marks that, and both do make a motion / unto a third," as Herbert observes in *The H. Scriptures* (II), grasps the undertones of qualification sounded by the imagery. In yet other poems, those which closely resemble New Testament parables, general language is the inevitable vehicle for the universal dramatic situations. Herbert seems fond of imitating the elements of these Biblical *exempla*—the archetypal situations, the husbandman-vine and lord-steward motifs, the slight interpretation of the narrative. Many of his imitations have a Biblical aura: "Having been tenant long to a rich Lord" *(Redemption)*, "My stock lies dead, and no increase / doth my dull husbandrie improve" *(Grace)*, "I made a posy while the day ran by" *(Life)*, "I blesse thee, Lord, because I Grow / among thy trees" *(Paradise)*, "I travell'd on, seeing the hill, where lay / my expectation" *(The Pilgrimage)*, "When God at first made man, / having a glasse of blessings standing by" *(The Pulley)*, "Come ye hither All, whose taste / is your waste, / save your cost, and mend your fare / God is here prepar'd and drest" *(The Invitation)*, "My Lord, if writing may convey / a Lordship any way" *(Obedience)*. Just as Herbert's Biblical models set forth their highly typical situations in general words which expand infinitely in meaning, many poems in *The Temple* rely for their effect on language which spreads out to include everyman in their implication. Generality of language, then, marks no fuzziness of idea.

Yet while much of the vocabulary of *The Temple* is designedly general, much of it is indisputedly simple. Herbert prefers the short and familiar word, especially when he is concerned with the most profound issues and is engaged in the most searching exploration of the spirit. It is not uncommon for whole poems to contain only monosyllables and disyllables, and for those to be words which might crop up in casual speech. Everyone remembers their dominance in *Vertue, Discipline, Bitter-sweet, The Call,* and *Hope.* Herbert was not alone among seventeenth-century poets, of course, in using the short word effectively. Perhaps we can understand his practice more fully if we consider wherein it differs from those of other men of his time. Traherne, notably, couches many of his verse meditations in the most childlike and innocent of words which convey the sense of marvel with which his speaker perceives the visual splendors of the natural world. Usually, however, he sets these sights in a theological perspective by including a patently adult, theoretical word or so in the ingenuous exclamations. A considerable part of his effect arises from the ambivalence created by such words: innocence of observation thereby receives maturity of commentary. In the first stanza of *Wonder,* for example, he calculatedly produces a small shock, as well as added dimension, through the introduction of the somewhat incongruous word *Eternitie*:

> How like an Angel came I down!
>   How Bright are all Things here!
> When first among his Works I did appear
>   O how their GLORY me did Crown?
> The World resembled his *Eternitie,*
>   In which my Soul did Walk;
>   And ev'ry Thing that I did see,
>   Did with me talk.[7] [Italics Traherne's]

Or in the last strophe of *Eden,* the similarly artless statements of the opening lines are intellectualized by the explanation of the last clause:

> And [first enjoyments] were so Great, and so Divine,
> so Pure;
> So fair and Sweet,
> So True; when I did meet
> Them here at first, they did my Soul allure,
> And drew away my Infant feet
> Quite from the Works of Men; that I might see
> The Glorious Wonders of the DEITIE.[8]

Traherne, as these samples show, chose the small word to convey a sense of rational slightness, heightened by the contrastingly adult reflections upon innocence.

Herrick, also, could manage the simple word with great skill. Like Traherne, he used it in the service of simplicity; but unlike his fellow parson, he made it work to imply narrowness of subject matter or the trifling differences between one man and another—never restriction of sensibility. Wishing, for example, to inscribe an epitaph for himself which would show that death is supremely common, he writes:

> Thus I
> Passe by,
> And die:
> As One,
> Unknown,
> And Gon:
> I'm made,
> A shade,
> And laid
> I'th grave,
> There have
> My Cave.
> Where tell
> I dwell,
> *Farewell. (Upon his departure hence)*[9]

In *His Grange, or private wealth,* littleness of language
appears in decorous imitation of the unsophisticated character of his country pleasures:

> Though Clock,
> To tell how night drawes hence, I've none,
>   A Cock,
> I have, to sing how day drawes on.
>   I have
> A maid (my *Prew*) by good luck sent,
>   To save
> That little, Fates me gave or lent.
>   A Hen
> I keep, which creeking day by day,
>   Tells when
> She goes her long white egg to lay.
>
>   .   .   .   .   .
>
>   Which are
> But toyes, to give my heart some ease:
>   Where care
> None is, slight things do lightly please.[10]

Herbert's words, while frequently as short and commonplace as Herrick's and Traherne's, do not convey either
of their sorts of simplicity, or, I think, any kind of simplicity at all. Rather they are selected with an eye to making
the topics of meditation of *The Temple*—topics which can
be accurately styled metaphysical—seem as matter-of-fact
and as familiar as any item of everyday routine. Whereas
Traherne recounts his impressions of the other world in
terms of such qualities as *felicity, immanent influence, substantial light, infinity,* and *supersubstantial objects,* Herbert, whose purpose is to divest Heaven of any shred of
exoticism, describes it in terms remarkable only for their
earthliness. He speaks of celestial matters with such immediacy that one is convinced of their propinquity; heaven
seems as palpable as the boxes and cabinets which, like
heaven, hold desirable things, or as the flowers, which, like

God's abode, are bright and sweet. To Herbert Heaven seemed not only conceptually real, but actual and constantly accessible; he appears to have had the ability which he ascribes to pre-lapsarian Adam, "To heav'n from Paradise go, / as from one room t'another" (*The H. Communion*). The ease and joy with which he thinks of such journeys prompts the informality of his language. One who knows God very well can speak of Him in familiar terms.

That is not to imply that Herbert's speaking says little. Just as a skillful musical performer can render a Mozart etude with apparent ease, Herbert expresses complex ontological theses with both limpidity and modesty. Consider, for example, the first stanza of *Even-song*:

> Blest be the God of love,
> Who gave me eyes, and light, and power this day,
> Both to be busie, and to play.
> But much more blest be God above,
> Who gave me sight alone,
> Which to himself he did denie:
> For when he sees my waies, I dy:
> But I have got his sonne, and he hath none. (63)

Here is the sparest of language Herbert gives astonishingly comprehensive thanks for the temporal and spiritual blessings of the day, blessings which, by implication, should be acknowledged anew each evening. This poem, the last of a group of seven beginning with *Whitsunday*, like its companion pieces, interprets certain of the Propers for Whitsuntide. The initial stanza presents a variation of the Gospel for the Monday in Whitsunweek, in Herbert's time, as in our own, perhaps the most widely quoted Biblical summary of world history:

So God loved the world, that he gave his only begotten son, that whosoever believeth in him, should not perish, but have everlasting life. For God sent not his son into the world to condemn the world, but that the world through him might be saved. He that believeth on him is not condemned. But he that believeth not, is condemned already, because he hath not believed in the name of the only begotten son of God. And this is the condemnation: that light is come into the world, and men loved darkness more than light, because their deeds were evil. For every one that evil doth, hateth the light, neither cometh to the light, lest his deeds should be reproved. But he that doth truth cometh to the light, that his deeds may be known, how that they are wrought in God.

The opening of *Even-song* picks out most of the elements of the Gospel and combines them with a general thanksgiving for the events of the day. Certainly an evening prayer is the ideal occasion for meditation on this passage, for the poet can plausibly touch upon both light and darkness. (In subsequent stanzas of the poem, Herbert voices his gratitude for God's loving gift of darkness and rest, in evident contrast to the darkness of evil cited in the Fourth Gospel, but in the first stanza, the subject is light.) God loves the world enough, we learn in the three initial lines, to give His creatures sunlight, eyes to perceive the light, and energy to act upon the objects that they see; man's daily existence, then, is a divine blessing. The greater gift, however, surety of soul, occupies the poet's attention in the last five lines. The God of love is even more to be praised for sending the spiritual sun—and this for two reasons. The pitch of God's love in this gift is that He denied Himself the pleasure of His Son so that man might have inner enlightenment; God, then, has given man more than He has kept for Himself. Almost sportively, Herbert typifies the Redemption as God's blindness resultant from the giving away of the sun-Son: before the Incarnation, He looked at man, and so could see his unforgivable faults; since the advent of Christ, however, man looks at God, not the opposite, and so attains mercy and everlasting life, not the death which he deserves if impartially judged.

This stanza, a devotional expression at once witty and profound, attains its intimacy and confidence of tone largely because of the extreme simplicity of its language.

Paradise, to move to one other piece of verbal simplicity, has frequently been underestimated, probably because of its combination of simple words and a paring away of the letters of the ultimate words in each of the first lines, a kind of mimesis likely to strike many contemporary readers as outrageous gimmickry.

> I blesse thee, Lord, because I GROW
> Among thy trees, which in a ROW
> To thee both fruit and order OW.
>
> What open force, or hidden CHARM
> Can blast my fruit, or bring me HARM,
> While the inclosure is thine ARM?
>
> Inclose me still for fear I START.
> Be to me rather sharp and TART,
> Then let me want thy hand & ART.
>
> When thou dost greater judgements SPARE,
> And with thy knife but prune and PARE,
> Ev'n fruitfull trees more fruitful ARE.
>
> Such sharpnes shows the sweetest FREND:
> Such cuttings rather heal then REND:
> And such beginnings touch their END.   (132-33)

Herbert has done much, much more than simply devise five tercets which repetitiously dramatize the principle of pruning. The poem is, like several others in *The Temple,* a meditation on the Fortunate Fall, and throughout one finds tacit comparison of the material perfection of the Garden of Eden and its spiritual counterpart, Heaven. The ambiguous title indicates the two arms of the parallel. Early in the poem it becomes clear that the neatly ranked trees, so strongly reminiscent of the earthly paradise, are not fixtures of that innocent locale, for they flourish because of affliction. In the first strophe the inhabitant of

Paradise is shown paradoxically to grow despite physical diminution; he, like the vine of the parable, brings forth fruit. In the second, the garden is strongly associated with the Church, which Herbert in *Affliction* (V) praises as superior to the planted Garden of Eden: it is said to be enclosed. For Anglicans of Herbert's time, the enclosed garden stood as a familiar allegorical equivalent of the Church, since in Canticles 4:12 it was one of the metaphors applied to the bride ("A garden inclosed is my sister, my spouse; a spring shut up, a fountain sealed. Thy plants are an orchard of pomegranates, with pleasant fruits").[11] The man within the enclosure of the Church, then, need fear no alien adversary. Yet he should not expect uninterrupted tranquility, we learn in the third stanza, the unruffled changelessness of an Eden, for God Himself will be sharp to His trees; but comfortingly, all sharpness and tartness felt by the members of the Church will be benevolently instituted by the Husbandman. God's art of keen pruning improves upon nature, just as one's ascension from nature to grace can come about only through successful experiencing of trials and tests. Herbert concludes by pointing up the expectations of the pruned tree. It, more than the untouched tree of Eden, can perceive the sweetness of God; it is healed of maladies untouched in the natural tree; and it looks forward to an end more glorious than does the plant which will continue only in its natural state. Simplicity of language, yes; thinness of conception, no.

For a man who left no critical treatise, Herbert had a great deal to say about the writing of verse. Several of his pronouncements have been interpreted as declarations of his own simplicity and as proscriptions of what we now call metaphysical poetry. It is difficult to credit the idea that the maker of undeniably metaphysical poems could object seriously to the conceit, or that some of his conceits parody existing metaphysical verse, or that his early irritation with it gave way to approval: both early and late poems in *The Temple* demonstrate his reliance on almost every characteristic of the manner which some readers find him condemning. On the contrary, I feel, Herbert preached exactly what he practiced. He never made wholesale censure of embellishment in the writing of others and never disclaimed the complexity of his own work. I do not believe that one can find in Herbert any intimation that "writing from the heart" necessitates writing without the head.

He advocated writing from the heart, of course, and the terms in which he did so have since been misread. In the Jordan duo, notably, where he comes out sternly against poems which only pretend emotion, and so which must dress up their hollowness with painted veils, he speaks approvingly of plainness.

> I envie no mans nightingale or spring;
> Nor let them punish me with losse of rime,
>   Who plainly say, *My God, My King.* (57)

> My thoughts began to burnish, sprout, and swell,
> Curling with metaphors a plain intention,
> Decking the sense, as if it were to sell.
>
>   .   .   .   .   .
>
> But while I bustled, I might heare a friend
> Whisper, *How wide is all this long pretense!*
> *There is in love a sweetnesse readie penn'd:*
> *Copie out onely that, and save expense.* (102-103)

We must not confuse the quality here lauded with any modern concept of plainness involving thinness, absence of adornment, or naiveté. Verbal plainness for Herbert always was the vehicle of sincerity and sharpness of expression; its antithesis was not beauty or intricacy of idea, but pretension and imagerial clutter. The nightingale and spring incurring his disfavor in *Jordan* (I) do so because they are companionate to *fictions onely and false hair,* and the metaphors scorned in *Jordan* (I) offend him because they are *a long pretense,* a falsifying of the plain intention of devotion.

Nor, as he makes clear elsewhere, does he think that plainness of style excludes wit. In *The Church-porch,* he offers suggestions for the proper cultivation of that faculty, concluding with an admonition to plainness:

> Pick out of mirth, like stones out of thy ground,
> Profanenesse, filthinesse, abusivenesse,
> These are the scumme, with which course wits abound:
> The fine may spare these well, yet not go lesse,
>   All things are bigge with jest: nothing that's plain
>   But may be wittie, if thou hast the vein. (16)

In yet other poems plainness is associated with logic and truth. Speaking in *Dotage* of the palpable miseries of human life, he characterizes them as "Plain demonstrations, evident and cleare, / Fetching their proofs ev'n from the very bone. . . ." (167) And in *The Foil,* stars shine *plainly*:

> If we could see below
> The sphere of vertue, and each shining grace
>   As plainly as that above doth show;
> This were the better skie, the brighter place. (175)

Plainness, then, does not imply sensuous or intellectual poverty; how could it, if it is suitable for copying out the sweetness of God's love, a quantity which Herbert felt beyond the capacities of most philosophers to imagine?[12] Rather it is the fit attendant of earnestness, reasonableness, and integrity of statement.

Several times, Herbert expresses the intention of including the whole universe in his poetry and of ordering this magnitude of material with as much care as God has exercised in the imponderable balancing of the cosmos. In *The Dedication* he declares that he will vie with all of God's gifts in praise:

Lord, my first fruits present themselves to thee;
Yet not mine neither; for from thee they came,
And must return. Accept of them and me,
And make us strive, who shall sing best thy name. (5)

A tall order, to compete with the heavens which declare the glory of God, and with the firmament, which shows His handiwork (the allusion, I take it, in the fourth line)— surely a purpose to be pursued with all of the available skills of mimesis. He makes a similar avowal in *Praise* (II):

Wherefore with my utmost art
    I will sing thee,
And the cream of all my heart
    I will bring thee.

.   .   .   .   .

Small it is, in this poore sort
    To enroll thee:
Ev'n eternitie is too short
    To extoll thee. (146)

Again in *Christmas,* he promises the enlistment of all of his capacities in the making of song for God:

The shepherds sing; and shall I silent be?
    My God, no hymne for thee?
My soul's a shepherd too; a flock it feeds
    Of thoughts, and words, and deeds.
The pasture is thy word; the streams, thy grace
    Enriching all the place.
Shepherd and flock shall sing, and all my powers
    Out-sing the day-light hours. (81)

It is in *The Forerunners* that Herbert makes his most detailed statement about metaphor and about its function in poetry. Ruefully conjecturing that the clever inventions of his brain might escape with the increasing whitening of his hair, leaving him with only the meditation of his heart, *Thou are still my God,* he feels no anxiety that God will reject this hymn, since the prime impetus of poetry, the heartfelt sentiment, remains:

> Good men ye be, to leave me my best room,
> Ev'n all my heart, and what is lodged there:
> I passe not, I, what of the rest become,
> So *Thou art still my God,* be out of fear.
>   He will be pleased with that dittie;
> And if I please him, I write fine and wittie. (176)

Yet he regrets the possible departure of beautiful and witty tropes, since they have been his best and have been duly presented to God:

> Farewell sweet phrases, lovely metaphors,
> But will ye leave me thus? when ye before
> Of stews and brothels onely knew the doores,
> Then did I wash you with my tears, and more,
>   Brought you to Church well drest and clad:
> God must have my best, ev'n all I had.

> Lovely enchanting language, sugar-cane,
> Hony of roses, whither wilt thou flie?
> Hath some fond lover tic'd thee to thy bane?
> And wilt thou leave the Church, and love a stie?
>   Fie, thou wilt soil thy broider'd coat,
> And hurt thyself, and him that sings the note.

Left to him now is *my best room, | Ev'n all my heart, and what is lodged there;* formerly, however, when his capacities of brain and heart were at their fullest, the Christianizing of the whole range of profane verse, the washing and dressing of its language and imagery, were *my best, ev'n all I had,* with the wit and heart working together. God, then, accepts the simple song of the devoted heart when the inventive faculty is dull, but it is the duty of the accomplished poet to engage all of the embellishments at his command when he undertakes to write praises. As Herbert comments later in the poem, "Beautie and beauteous words should go together." Certainly they did in *The Temple*.

One or two other poems embody apologies for such simplicity—that forced by ingenuousness—but, like *The Forerunners*, they intimate that more than simplicity is exacted of the man of superior discernment. In *A true Hymne*, the speaker laments his ability to devise more than three devotional phrases: *My joy, my life, my crown*. Then it comforts him to reflect that, if the three phrases are truly all that the loving worshipper can muster, God stands ready to finish the hymn:

> Yet slight not these few words:
> If truly said, they may take part
> Among the best in art.
> The finenesse which a hymne or psalme affords,
> Is, when the soul unto the lines accords.
>
> .   .   .   .   .
>
> Whereas if th' heart be moved,
> Although the verse be somewhat scant,
> God doth supplie the want.
> As when th' heart sayes (sighing to be approved)
> *O could I love!* and stops: God writeth, *Loved*. (168)

But notice that God supplies a want. The artless phrases are acceptable because heartfelt, but they do not represent the desideratum of sacred poetry, any more than does the bleak paleness of writing which is left the aging protagonist at the conclusion of *The Forerunners*. In both poems, simplicity is held defensible under certain circumstances, but is not postulated as the goal for which the dedicated poet should strive. He should, rather, as Herbert affirms in *Dulnesse*, marshall all of his apprehensive faculties, so that he may utter worthy praise:

> O give me quicknesse, that I may with mirth
> Praise thee brim-full!
>
> .   .   .   .   .

> Lord, cleare thy gift, that with a constant wit
> I may but look towards thee:
> *Look* onely; for to *love* thee, who can be,
> What angel fit? (115-16)

In *Sion,* a groan is found to be more pleasing to God than
the perfunctory ceremoniousness practiced in Solomon's
temple; yet groans as music, we learn in *Gratefulnesse,* are
but *countrey-aires.* Herbert was not satisfied to produce
country airs. He pledged his utmost art. And even that
was not enough. Even the adoration of men and angels in
consort, we are told at the conclusion of *Antiphon* (II),
falls short of what God deserves. With such an aspiring
conception of divine poetry as Herbert's professed guide,
we should not scan *The Temple* for devotions of childlike
piety or of highly polished simplicity. Herbert put into his
verse *ev'n all I had.* For a man of his breeding, learning,
and sensibility, this all was a vast amount.

The most important element of all, however, was
purity of heart. And it is this very luminosity of spirit
which has done Herbert much disservice in our time, for,
as Helen C. White has so perceptively observed, many
modern readers insist, as seventeenth-century men did not,
upon innocence as a prerequisite of intense piety.[13] Herbert's piety is overwhelmingly evident in every single page
of *The Temple,* more so, certainly, than the wit and learning which he believed ancillary to sanctity. It is a kind of
simplicity on our part, as well as a myopia, if, noting that
Herbert is genuinely holy, we insist upon reading his verse
as jejune. For its primary impact to be one of lowly-
hearted praise is precisely what he intended; and a refusal
to recognize that a well-equipped adult mind has been
painstakingly disciplined to make this humility possible
springs from our obstinacy, not Herbert's deficiency. One
is ready to read *The Temple* with understanding only
when he appreciates the fact that the poet has not
repressed his apprehension of this world in writing of the

next, but that he has drawn upon the materials of intellect, sense, tradition, and experience, and has with utmost art ordered these materials into expressions of unswerving faith. The Fall of Man, which Herbert repeatedly appraised as fortunate, enabled man to regard God with awareness and with understanding, and thus to be capable of some estimate of His greatness. Herbert's awareness and understanding, the chief instruments by which he measures heavenly omniscience, instruments consequently indivisible from his humility, contribute immeasurably to *The Temple*.

Appendix: Herbert and William Alabaster

THE RESEMBLANCES between Herbert's devotional verse and William Alabaster's sonnets seem to me sufficiently close to suggest that Herbert was acquainted with the English poetry of Alabaster, which he might have seen in manuscript in the Cambridge library. Much of the likeness —its really important quotient—is too subjective to lend itself to neat demonstration: both men achieve a tone of unpretentious intimacy with the deity whom they address, equally unlike the delicately romantic artifice of Southwell and the man-to-man forthrightness of Donne, to mention two other early religious writers of the metaphysical manner; both revitalize medieval materials through the infusion of "modern" secular detail; and both concentrate a considerable variety of materials into short poems of deceptively smooth surface. While the combination of these characteristics is far from usual for the time, it scarcely proves that Herbert read Alabaster's English verse. Yet one can point to a number of specific parallels which warrant the supposition that Herbert might indeed have encountered the Cambridge MS. and so have seen the *I sing of Christ* sonnet. Both Alabaster's Sonnet 20 *(Resurrection)* and Herbert's *The Discharge* contain the highly unusual figure of the present as the nexus of two bottoms (spools of thread), the loose end of the first initiating the

winding of the second. Alabaster's Sonnet 22, which celebrates Easter morning, immediately calls up *Easter-wings*
to the Herbert aficionado; it meditatively associates sinful
man with Christ in His death and descent, and the ability
of man to rise from his sin because of the Resurrection.
Moreover, it, like *Easter-wings,* charts the descent-ascent
movement twice, once in the octave, once in the sestet
("Sink down, my soul, into the lowest cell, . . . Rise up, my
soul, as high as God doth dwell"; "Descend in patience
with him to die, / Ascend in confidence with him to reign").
In Sonnet 24, Alabaster speculates on how he can most
eloquently express the greatness of his heavenly theme.
He comes to two conclusions: that simplicity is best ("Thus
plainly will I write: no sin like mine"); and that Christ will
approve and almost write for the man of earnest heart
("Then be thy spirit the quill, / thy blood the ink, and
with compassion / write thus upon my soul: thy Jesu still").
These lines might well have been written by Herbert.
They are, I think, particularly close in both sentiment and
specificity of expression to the conclusion of *Jordan* (I)
("Nor let them punish me with losse of rime, / Who plainly
say, *My God, My King*"), and to that of *A true Hymne,*
where Herbert again sanctions spareness of style:

> Whereas if th' heart be moved,
> Although the verse be somewhat scant,
> God doth supplie the want.
> As when th' heart sayes (sighing to be approved)
> *O, could I love!* and stops: God writeth, *Loved.* (168)

The beginning of Sonnet 32 *(Upon the Crucifix)* ("Behold
a vine . . . whose grapes do swell with grace and heavenly
lustre") verbally parallels the familiar first stanza of *Jordan*
(II), in which Herbert explains that when he first wrote
of *heav'nly* joys, his lines had such *lustre,* that they did
sprout and *swell.* The octave of Sonnet 48 is almost a
microcosm of *The Pearl:*

Lord, I have left all and myself behind,
My state, my hopes, my strength, and present ease,
My unprovoked studies' sweet disease,
And touch of nature and engrafted kind,
Whose cleaving twist doth distant tempers bind,
And gentle sense of kindness that doth praise
The earnest judgements, others' wills to please:
All and myself I leave thy love to find.

Sonnet 50 makes the same distinction between the sun shining through clear glass and through stained glass that Herbert employs in *The Windows*:

But as the sun beams though they be bright,
Through coloured glass like colour do reflect,
So doth the person's misconceit infect:
My comfort, clear in me, in you is night.

Sonnet 61 bears strong resemblance to *The Pulley*. In the earlier poem, Alabaster, like Herbert in his pawkier fable, shows God giving man a multitude of blessings, only to discover that man enjoyed the gifts but had forgotten the Giver, then having to cast about to find a means of luring His creature back to Himself:

God was in love with man, and sued then
To get return of love by all those ways
Which lovers use to compass in their praise.
His image he did draw with nature's pen,
To show his beauty and his worth to men;
His tokens were all good, that our life says;
His agents were the prophets that did raise
Man's heart to love where he had loved been.
But man did love the gift, and not the giver,
Yet see how God did in his love persever:
He gave himself, that as a gift he might
Be loved by taking, putting on our feature
So to be seen in more familiar sight.
How must we love him that so loves his creature!

Herbert, of course, alters God's solution, but the process of reasoning by which He arrives at withholding rest from man almost repeats that of the Alabaster poem:

> For if I should (said he)
> Bestow this jewell also on my creature,
> He would adore my gifts in stead of me,
> And rest in Nature, not the God of Nature:
> So both should losers be. (160)

Both poets typify John the Beloved Disciple at the Last Supper as sucking divinity from Christ's bosom, and express their own wish to do likewise. In Sonnet 77:

> High towering eagle . . . at his Supper didst lean
> on his breast.
> Boldness of love upon his breast to lie,
> And there didst suck of his divinity,
> Which in thy heavenly gospel is expressed.
> . . . I not only on thy breast will lean
> But through thy breast unto thy heart will run
> Is that such boldness? Therefore it was riven.

And similarly from Herbert's *Lucus*:

> Ah, nunc, helluo, fac, vt ipse sugam:
> Num totum tibi pectus imputabis?
> Fontem intercipis omnibus patentem?
> Quin pro me quoque sanguinem profudit,
> Et ius pectoris inde consecutus
> Lac cum sanguine posco deuolutum;
> Vt, si gratia tanta copuletur
> Peccati veniae mei, vel ipsos
> Occumbens humero Thronos lacessam. (421)

Trans. Ah, now glutton, grant that I may suck. Will you keep the whole bosom for yourself? Do you cut off the fountain open to all? Truly He shed blood for me, too, and I, consequently, demand the milk of that bosom flowing down with blood; until, when such favor is joined with forgiveness of my sin, I may even—lying on his shoulder—challenge the thrones themselves.

These likenesses, all involving more or less uncommon ideas, images, or words, convince me that Herbert had indeed seen the Alabaster MS. deposited in his University library and, moreover, had gone through it with attention and respect. If so, then he would have known the *I sing of Christ* sonnet, a "metaphysical" resolution to turn the devices of the ancients to the praise of God.

Notes

INTRODUCTION

1 Gilbert Thomas, "George Herbert," *Contemporary Review,* CXLIII (1933), 707.

2 F. E. Hutchinson, ed., *The Works of George Herbert* (Oxford, 1941); Rosamund Tuve, *A Reading of George Herbert* (Chicago, 1952); Joseph Summers, *George Herbert: His Religion and Art* (London, 1954); Marchette Chute, *Two Gentle Men: The Lives of George Herbert and Robert Herrick* (New York, 1959). Margaret Bottrall's *George Herbert* (London, 1954) is an appreciative and uniformly perceptive descant on various aspects of the verse, but does not (nor does it attempt to) add substantially to our apprehension of the thematic materials.

CHAPTER I

1 See Palmer's introduction to his edition of *The English Works of George Herbert* (Boston, 1905), I, 166; Williamson, *The Donne Tradition* (Cambridge, 1930), p. 109; Warren, "George Herbert," *American Review,* VII (1936), 270; Bush, *Mythology and the Renaissance Tradition in English Poetry* (New York, 1957), p. 226; Joseph Summers, *George Herbert: His Religion and Art* (London, 1954), p. 113; Marchette Chute, *Two Gentle Men: The Lives of George Herbert and Robert Herrick* (New York, 1959), p. 113.

2 Beatrice Johnson, in a regrettably neglected article, has pointed out about thirty Donne poems incorporating classical materials ("Classical Allusions in the Poetry of Donne," *PMLA,* XLIII [1928], 1098-1109); more recently, E. E. Duncan-Jones has cited Virgil as the source of the barren plane tree in *The Autumnal* ("The Barren Plane Tree in Donne's Autumnal," *Notes and Queries,* n.s. VII [1960], 53). I find

the following allusions: to the Sirens (commonly called mermaids in his time) in *Goe and catch a falling starre;* Phoebus and the Hours, Days, and Months in *The Sunne Rising;* Venus in *The Indifferent;* the God of Love in *Loves Usury;* the eagle, dove, and phoenix in *The Canonization;* the Sun (winged and spurred) in *Sweetest love, I do not goe;* the Sybils, Pindar, Lucan, Homer, and the God of Love in *A Valediction: of the Booke;* the Sun in *Loves Growth;* the blind and childish God of Love in *Loves exchange;* primal Chaos, the Sun, and the Zodiac in *A Nocturnall upon S. Lucies Day;* the vestal virgins in *The Apparition;* the God of Love and Jove in *Loves Deitie;* Argus in *The Will*—all from *Songs and sonets.* Three of the epigrams deal with mythological topics *(Hero and Leander, Pyramus and Thisbe,* and *Nobbe);* here, also, one finds references to the Sun in *Sir John Winge-field;* Martial in *Raderus;* and Aesop and Mercury in *Mercurius Gallo-Belgicus.* Over half of the elegies contain classical motifs: the cocka-trĭce, the unicorn, and the colossus of Rhodes in IV; Chaos, Cynthia, Prosperpine, Jove, and Mount Aetna in VIII; the Golden Age and Xerxes and his Lydian love in IX; Cynthia, Venus, Chaos, the God of Love, Venus' dove, Justice, Phoebus, and Fortune in XII; the Mantuan, the Chymera, and Orcus in XIII; Boreas, Orithyia, and Jove in XVI; the God of Love with his wings and bow in XVII; Cupid, Pluto, the ambrosial islands, the Sirens, the Delphic oracle, the cleaving Ramora, the Hellespont, and Sestos and Abydos in XVIII; Atalanta in XIX; and Midas in XX. In imitation of Ovid he wrote an heroical epistle, *Sapho to Philaenis.* Classical materials occur in all four of his epithala-mia: one finds the halcyon bird, the phoenix, and satyrs in *On the Lady Elizabeth and County Palatine;* Flora and Cupid in *Ecclogue;* the Sun, Prometheus, the Muses, Phaeton, and Tully in *Epithalamion* (1613); Flora, the Senators and patricians, the Hermaphrodite, Phoebus, and the amorous evening star in *Epithalamion made at Lincolnes Inne.* Among the satires one finds the Muses in I; Coscus, Carthusian fasts, and Bachanalls in II; the salamander and Phrygius in III; the Spartans, Caesar's histories, Circe, the Sun, and Heraclitus in IV; the Muses, the iron age, Destiny, Fate, and Aesop in V; Caesar's histories, and the Sybils in *Upon Mr. Thomas Coryats Cruditiis.* Among the verse letters appear the Fates and Fortune in *To Mr. Christopher Brooke: The Storme;* Chaos in *To Sir Henry Wotton;* the Sun and the Fates in *To the Countesse of Bedford: Madame, you have refin'd;* Jove, Diana, and the Muses in *To the Countesse of Bedford: T'have written then;* the Zodiac and planets named for the gods in *To the Countesse of Hunt-ingdon: Madame, man to Gods image;* Nature, Fortune, and the Muses in *To Mr. T. W.: All haile sweet Poet;* the Muses in *To Mr. R. W.: Zealously my Muse;* Parnassus in *To Mr. E. G.;* Morpheus in *To Mr. R. W.: If, as mine is;* Echo in *To Mr. R. W.: Kindly I envy;* Helicon and the Sirens in *To Mr. S. B.;* Lethe and the Muses in *To Mr. I. L.: Of that short Roll of friends;* the Muses in *To Mr. B. B.;* Fortune in *To Sir H. W. at his going Ambassador to Venice;* the allegory of the cave in *To the Countesse of Salisbury. The First Anniversary,* of course, makes extended use of Astrea; it also contains mentions of the Muses, Fate, the Pigmies, the Phoenix, the Zodiac, and the Iron Age. In *A Funerall Elegie* one finds Fate and Destiny; in *The Second Anniversary,* the Muses, Lethe, the Golden Age, Mithridates, Fortune, the allegory of the newly-hatched soul, Venus, Argus, Mercury, Mars, Jove, Cicero, and Caesar. Fate, Pompey, and the Muses figure in *Obsequies to the Lord Harrington;* the fifth emperor and the gods and goddesses in *Death;* Janus, Destiny, the Roman Empire, the Colossus, Morea, Jove, the Sun, the Zodiac, and the emperors in *The Progresse of the Soule;* a crown of bays in *La Corona* I; Fate in V; the Muses in VII. Donne, like Aeneas, braves the mouth of hell to see his father in the seventh of the holy sonnets; one finds Lethe in the ninth; the dove of Venus in the eighteenth; the Zodiac in *The Litanie;* the Hermaphrodite in *To Mr. Tilman after he had taken orders.*

3 See Edward Dowden, *Puritan and Anglican: Studies in Literature* (New York, 1901), p. 107.

4 Helen C. White, *The Metaphysical Poets: A Study in Religious Experience* (New York, 1936), p. 166.

5 Summers, pp. 86 ff.

6 John David Walker, "The Architectonics of George Herbert's *The Temple,*" *ELH,* XXIX (1962), 289-305, esp. p. 290.

7 See F. E. Hutchinson's introduction to his edition of *The Works of George Herbert* (Oxford, 1941), pp. lxx-lxxiv.

8 One other serious objection to his thesis might be mentioned. He looks upon *The Church-porch* as a symbolic baptism, in keeping, he feels, with the sprinkling imagery of the *Perirrhanterium* and *Superliminare.* In Jewish practice, however, baptism occurred only when proselytes were converted to Judaism. For an authoritative discussion of these rites, see George Foot Moore, *Judaism in the First Centuries of the Christian Era* (Cambridge, 1927), I, 332 ff.

9 Ben Jonson, *The Poems,* ed. B. H. Newdigate (Oxford, 1936), p. 269.

10 All Herbert quotations are from Hutchinson's edition and are identified by appropriate page numbers.

11 A. D., "Five Notes on George Herbert," *Notes and Queries,* CXCVII (1952), 420-22.

12 Quoted from *The Greek Anthology,* ed. W. R. Paton, Loeb Classical Library, V, 65.

13 See Robert Herrick, *Poetical Works,* ed. F. W. Moorman (Oxford, 1915), pp. 256-57.

[14] William Alabaster, *Sonnets,* ed. G. M. Story and Helen Gardner, Oxford English Monographs (Oxford, 1959), p. 30. I quote the whole of this sonnet because I believe that Herbert had seen the Alabaster verse and that this particular sonnet might have been his credo in *The Temple.* Herbert does indeed enrobe his thoughts with the ornaments of many worlds, just as Alabaster proposed to do. See the Appendix for further parallels between Alabaster and Herbert.

[15] *Divine Weekes and Workes* (London, 1633).

[16] Christopher Harvey, *Complete Poems,* ed. A. B. Grosart (London, 1874).

[17] For information about the shaped poem, I am much indebted to Margaret Church's *The Pattern Poem* (an unpublished Radcliffe Dissertation, 1944).

[18] Quoted in Church, p. 278.

[19] William Browne, *Poems,* ed. Gordon Goodwin (London, 1894), II, 142.

[20] *A Political Rhapsody,* ed. Hyder Edward Rollins (Cambridge, Mass., 1931), I, 122.

[21] Hutchinson, p. 484.

[22] See *The H. Communion.*

[23] *Patrologia Latina,* II, 84-85.

[24] Quoted in DeWitt T. Starnes and Earnest William Talbert, *Classical Myth and Legend in Renaissance Dictionaries* (Chapel Hill, 1955), p. 270.

[25] A famous parallel to the same words occurs in the first chapter of the *Confessions* of St. Augustine, one of the two authors whom Herbert valued sufficiently to mention in his will among the others represented in his library. Perhaps Herbert had in mind the *Confessions* rather than the Gospel: "*Tu excitas, ut te delectet: quia fecisti nos ad te, et inquietum est cor nostrum, donec requiescat in te . . .*" (*Patrologia Latina,* XXXII, 660).

[26] A. Davenport, "George Herbert and Ovid," *Notes and Queries,* n.s. II (1955), 98.

[27] See Sidney's *Come sleep! O sleep the certain knot of peace,* Daniel's *Care Charmer sleep, son of the sable night,* Bartholomew Griffin's *Care-charmer sleep, sweet ease in restless misery,* Drayton's *Black pitchy night, companion of my woe,* Beaumont and Fletcher's *Care-charming sleep, thou easer of all woes,* Drummond's *Sleep, silence' child, sweet father of soft rest.* See also lines 281-94 of Sackville's *Induction,* and Shakespeare's *II Henry IV* III.i.5 ff., *Henry V* IV.ii 280 ff., *Macbeth* II.ii.36 ff.

[28] Don Cameron Allen, *Image and Meaning: Metaphoric Traditions in Renaissance Poetry* (Baltimore, 1960), p. 69.

[29] See *Patrologia Latina,* CXIII, 110.

[30] For a discussion of the emblematic tradition of the crow as an attribute of hope, see Dora and Erwin Panofsky, *Pandora's Box* (Bollingen Series LII, New York, 1956), pp. 31-33.

[31] See Virgil, *Georgics* III.8; Quintillian 9.9.92; Spenser, *Visions of Bellay* 4.5; Crashaw, *Sospetto*, 28.6-8; Shakespeare, *Richard III*, V. iii.106; Herrick, *To the King, upon his taking of Leicester; Paradise Lost* VI. 762, II. 452.

[32] Quoted by A. B. Grosart, ed., *The Complete Works in Verse and Prose of George Herbert* (London, 1874), I, 283.

[33] G. Blakemore Evans, "George Herbert's 'Jordan,'" *Notes and Queries*, n.s. V (1958), 215.

[34] Rosamund Tuve, *A Reading of George Herbert*, p. 187.

[35] Roberta Florence Brinkley, ed., *English Poetry of the XVII Century* (New York, 1936), p. 256.

[36] *Complete Works*, ed. Albert Feuillerat (Cambridge, 1912-1926), III, 41-42.

[37] Sidney, II, 248-49.

[38] After I had arrived at my interpretation of this poem, I was delighted to find a gloss of the painted chair associating it with *Republic* X in the excellent new anthology edited by Hugh Kenner (*Seventeenth Century Poetry: The Schools of Donne and Jonson*, New York, 1964). Mr. Kenner and I "found" the meaning of this line quite independently, a fact which makes me less hesitant to expound the Platonic origin with great emphasis.

[39] Elbridge Colby, "The Echo Device in Literature," *Bulletin of the New York Public Library*, XXIII (1919), 683-713, 783-804. Reprinted in book form in 1920.

[40] See the introduction to his edition of *The Poems English and Latin of Edward Lord Herbert of Cherbury* (Oxford, 1923), p. xxix.

[41] Smith, p. 48.

[42] *Ovide Moralisée* (Modern Language Association of America Photographic Facsimile No. 326), p. 33.

[43] See, for example, the allusion in Barnabe Barnes' *A Divine Century of Spiritual Sonnets* (1595), quoted in J. William Hebel and Hoyt H. Hudson, eds., *Poetry of the English Renaissance* (New York, 1947), p. 217. Barnes wishes that his soul, blinded by dust, may march

> To that camp
> Of sacred soldiers whose protection
> He that victorious on a white horse rideth,
> Taketh, and evermore triumphant guideth.

[44] Quoted in Grosart, *Complete Works*, I, 235.

[45] Hutchinson, p. 477.

[46] Quoted in Grosart, *Complete Works*, I, 242.

[47] Glossed by Hutchinson, pp. 480-81.

48 Grosart, *Complete Works,* I, 267-68.

49 Diogenes Laertius, *Diogenes* 41, quoted in *Lives of Eminent Philosophers,* ed. R. D. Hicks, Loch Classical Library (London, 1925), II, 43.

50 F. J. Furnivall, ed., *Francis Thynne's Emblemes and Epigrames,* EETS, Vol. 33, No. 64 (London, 1876), pp. 9-10.

51 Furnivall, p. 36.

52 Herrick, p. 262. Richard Crashaw, *Poems,* ed. L. C. Martin (Oxford, 1927), p. 234; Thomas Carew, *Poems,* ed. Rhodes Dunlap (Oxford, 1949), p. 38.

53 See George Ferguson, *Signs & Symbols in Christian Art* (New York, 1954), p. 107.

54 Rosamund Tuve, "George Herbert and *Caritas,*" *Journal of the Warburg and Courtauld Institutes,* XXII (1959), 320.

55 Henry Vaughan, *Works,* ed. Leonard C. Martin (2d ed., Oxford, 1957), p. 462.

56 *Ovide Moralisée,* p. 218.

57 Notice the close approximation to a passage from Southwell's *The Prodigall Chyld's Soul Wracke,* quoted from C. M. Hood, *The Book of Robert Southwell* (Oxford, 1926), p. 108:

> They sought by theire bewitching charmes
> So to enchant my erring sense . . .
> With Syren's songs they feed my eares
> Till, lul'd asleepe in Error's lapp,
> I found these tunes turn'd into teares,
> And short delightes to long mishapp.

58 *Ovide Moralisée,* pp. 396-97.

59 Starnes and Talbert, pp. 109-10.

60 Palmer, II, 120.

61 See Davis P. Harding, *Milton and the Renaissance Ovid,* Illinois Studies in Language and Literature, Vol. 30, No. 4 (Urbana, 1946).

62 In *Psyche,* iii, stanza 102.

CHAPTER II

1 Throughout this discussion I shall use *pun* to indicate a wide range of verbal ambiguities, simply because it is the only modern term of which I am aware denoting the artful attachment of more than one meaning to a single word. During Herbert's time, several kinds of semantic ambiguity were distinguished. One may find them conveniently illustrated in Sister Miriam Joseph's *Shakespeare's Use of the Arts of Language* (New York, 1947), pp. 165-66. *Antanaclasis* is the investing of a single repeated word with two or more meanings;

syllepsis is the contrivance of making a single unrepeated word convey a double sense; *paronomasia* or *agomination* is the use of two phonologically similar words with different meanings. *Pun,* it seems to me, satisfactorily covers all of these figures.

2 Edward King's brother Henry, one of Milton's fellow contributors to the collection of obsequies, perceived the exact point of Herbert's poem and paraphrased it in the second of his two memorial verses. His brother, he boasts, had *not* divorced natural and divine truth:

> Whose active spirit so swift and clearly wrought
> Free from all dregs of earth, that you'd have thought
> His body were assum'd, and did disguise
> Some one of the celestiall Hierarchies.
> Whose reason quite *outstript* our faith, and knew
> What we are bound but to beleeve is true;
> Religion was but the position
> Of his own judgement, *truth to him alone*
> *Stood nak'd; he strung th' arts chain,* and knit the ends,
> And made divine and humane learning
>   friends. . . . (Italics mine)

Quoted from *Justa Edovardo King,* Facsimile Text Society, Publication No. 45 (New York, 1939), F 2.

3 Apparently the ark as a type of Christ evolved from early claims for the four lines of the ark signifying the four members of man, in conjunction with the association of Noah's ark with the ark of the covenant, the house of the tables of the law prefiguring Christ and the inner law. See Ambrose, *De Noe et Arca, Patrologia Latina,* XIV, 389-91.

4 A. D., "Five Notes on George Herbert," *Notes and Queries,* CXCVII (1952), 420-22.

5 Herbert himself used it again, again spelled as in *The Sacrifice,* in line thirty-three of *The Thanksgiving.* Vaughan realized the ambiguity of *The Sacrifice* and copied it in *Easter-day:*

> Arise, arise,
> And with his healing bloud anoint thine Eys,
>   Thy inward Eys; his bloud will cure thy mind,
>   Whose spittle only could restore the blind. (456)

6 Vaughan, it is worth noting, rendered this figure more explicit in *Faith,* which throughout echoes the Herbert poem:

> But as in nature, when the day
>   Breaks, night adjourns,
> Stars shut up shop, mists pack away,
>   And the moon mourns;

So when the Sun of righteousness
                Did once appear,
That Scene was chang'd, and a new dresse
                Left for us here. . . . (451)

7 John Hollander, *The Untuning of the Sky* (Princeton, 1961), p. 298.

8 A. D., *Notes and Queries,* CXCVII, 420-22.

9 See Hutchinson's note, p. 507.

10 Sir John Davies, *Poems,* ed. Clare Howard (New York, 1941), p. 156.

11 Davies, p. 155.

12 Herbert was fond of musical groans. He speaks of them in *Gratefulnesse, The Search, The Crosse,* and *Grieve not the Holy Spirit.*

13 A. B. Grosart, ed., *The Complete Works in Verse and Prose of George Herbert* (London, 1874), I, 303.

14 Grosart, I, 306; William Empson, *Seven Types of Ambiguity* (London, 1930), pp. 129-31.

15 A. D., *Notes and Queries,* CXCVII, 420-22.

16 Don Cameron Allen, *Image and Meaning: Metaphoric Traditions in Renaissance Poetry* (Baltimore, 1960), p. 69.

17 Grosart, I, 132.

18 The ambiguity is noted by Conrad Hilberry in his "Herbert's *Dooms-day,*" *Explicator,* XVI (1958), Item 24.

19 George Herbert Palmer, ed., *The English Works of George Herbert* (Boston, 1905), I, 165-66.

CHAPTER III

1 Rosamund Tuve, *A Reading of George Herbert* (Chicago, 1952), p. 145.

2 Tuve, p. 130.

3 Rosamund Tuve, "Sacred 'Parody' of Love Poetry, and Herbert," *Studies in the Renaissance,* VIII (1961), 249-88.

4 Herbert uses this pun again. In *Peace,* he recounts the multiplication of the twelve stalks of wheat which sprang from the grave of the Prince of Salem:

. . . They that taste it do rehearse,
                That vertue lies therein,
A secret vertue bringing peace and mirth
                By flight of sinne. (125)

In *Providence,* the double meaning appears again: "Who hath the vertue to expresse the rare / And curious vertues both of herbs and stones?" (119) And also in *Constancie:* "His goodnesse sets not, but in dark can runne: / The sunne to others writeth laws, / And is their vertue; Vertue is his Sunne." (72)

5 Quoted from Ronald B. McKerrow, ed., *The Works of Thomas Nashe* (2d ed., Oxford, 1958), III, 195.

6 John Cordy Jeaffreson, *A Book about the Clergy* (London, 1870), II, 249.

7 See *Conscience:* "And the receit shall be / My Saviours bloud: when ever at his board / I do but taste it, straight it cleanseth me. . . ." (106)

Love unknown: "I bath'd it often, ev'n with holy bloud, / Which at a board, while many drunk bare wine, / A friend did steal into my cup for good. . . ." (130)

Longing: "Thy board is full, yet humble guests / Finde nests." (149)

8 T. O. Mabbott, "Herbert's *The Collar*," *Explicator*, III (1945), Item 12; and Dan S. Norton, "Herbert's *The Collar*," *Explicator*, III (1945), Item 46.

9 G. P. V. Akrigg, "George Herbert's 'The Caller,'" *Notes and Queries*, n.s. I (1954), 17.

CHAPTER IV

1 Hutchinson gives an admirably full description of the Williams MS., p. lii ff.

2 Compare, for example, the Milky Way allusion in a letter to Launcelot Andrewes (p. 473) with that of *Prayer* (I); the death-in-nature imagery of the fifth poem of the *Memoriae Matris Sacrum* with that of *Vertue;* the architectural imagery of the first stanza of *Man* with that of *Sepulchre* and *Confession;* the comments upon hymning in *Praise* (I) and *Praise* (III).

3 Until I became interested in the frequency of Herbert's similes, I had not fully realized the vexations inherent in identifying that trope. Not all comparisons involving "like" or "as," obviously, are similes. "I will go as soon as I can" is not one, since the parallel which it draws is not figurative; "My lines and life are free; free as the rode" clearly is. Yet there are borderline cases which give one pause. What, for example, of "Was ever grief like mine"? Or of "As sinne came, so Sacraments might flow"? I suspect that the first, the refrain of *The Sacrifice*, makes a quite literal analogy and so should not be termed a simile, and that in the second, the *as* means *just as,* not *since,* and so denotes the trope. In numbering similes in Herbert and Donne I have, in questionable cases, tried to reckon only with the likenesses which are figurative. That Herbert might have envisioned the associations of Old Testament type and New Testament mystery as literal is, of course, a problem. I have assumed them to be

in some sense figurative and so have counted the comparisons involving them as similes.

4 Albert McHarg Hayes, "Counterpoint in Herbert," *SP*, XXXV (1938), 43-60.

5 He arranges the poems in seven groups: *harmonic*, in which the rhyme pattern and line lengths reinforce each other; *approximately harmonic*, with only one pair of lines lacking harmony; *isometrical*, in which all lines have the same length; *approximately contrapuntal stanzas*, in which only one pair of lines has harmony of line length and rhyme; *contrapuntal stanzas*, in which no rhyming lines have the same number of syllables; *off-balance stanzas*, in which one line is longer or shorter than the rest; *irregular stanzas*, "a motley group of miscellaneous patterns."

6 *Antiphon* (I), *Sighs and grones, Vertue, Home, The Quip, Businesse, Sinnes round, Love unknown, Clasping of hands, Praise* (III), *Dotage, Aaron,* and *The Posie.*

7 Early ones: *Easter, Love* (I) and (II), *Mattens, The World, The Pearl, Unkindnesse, Mortification, The H. Communion,* and *Prayer* (II); late ones: *The Agonie, Constancie, Sighs and grones, Vanitie* (I), *Vertue, Conscience, The Quip, The Dawning, Businesse, Sinnes round, The Call, Clasping of hands, Dotage, Aaron, The Invitation, The Banquet,* and *Dooms-day.*

8 Gene H. Koretz ("The Rhyme Scheme in Herbert's 'Man,'" *Notes and Queries,* n.s. III [1956], 144-46), proposed a (to me) unsatisfactory analysis of the plan. He comments that the poem consists of nine stanzas of six lines each; that nine is the square of three; that each stanza contains three pairs of rhyming lines and three pairs of lines of different lengths; and that this symmetry works with that of the symmetrically placed identical patterns of stanzas two and eight.

9 (1) *abccba*, (2) *abcabc*, (3) *abcbac*, (4) *abacbc*, (5) *aabcbc*, (6) *abaccb*, (7) *abbcac*, (8) *abcabc*, (9) *ababcc*.

10 Joseph Summers, *George Herbert: His Religion and Art* (London, 1954), p. 92.

CHAPTER V

1 See William Sloane, "George Herbert's Reputation, 1650-1710: Good Reading for the Young," *Notes and Queries,* CCVI (1962), 213.

2 T. S. Eliot, *George Herbert,* Writers and their Work No. 152 (London, 1962), p. 17.

3 Vaughan recognized this imagery of travel by water and imitated it, as well as other details of the poem (the journey through the wilderness, the sands and serpents), in *The Mutinie.*

4 See A. B. Chambers, "The Meaning of the 'Temple' in Donne's *La Corona*," *JEGP*, LIX (1959), 212-17.

5 See George Ferguson, *Signs & Symbols in Christian Art* (Oxford, 1954), p. 12.

6 See Rosemary Freeman, *English Emblem Books* (London, 1948), pp. 165 ff.

7 Thomas Traherne, *Poetical Works,* ed. Gladys I. Wade (London, 1932), p. 5.

8 Traherne, p. 7.

9 Robert Herrick, *Poetical Works,* ed. F. W. Moorman (Oxford, 1915), p. 178.

10 Herrick, p. 246.

11 Roman Catholics, of course, regarded the enclosed garden as a type of the Virgin.

12 So he says in the initial stanza of *The Agonie.*

13 Helen C. White, *The Metaphysical Poets. A Study in Religious Experience* (New York, 1936), p. 150.

Index

Herbert, George (*continued*):
plaining, 141, 142; *Confession*,
70, 164; *Conscience*, 127, 131,
139; *Constancie*, 52-53, 95-96,
139, 153, 192; *Content*, 97-98,
127, 135; *The Crosse*, 95, 116,
130; *The Dawning*, 127, 150;
Death, 49, 115, 127; *Decay*, 5;
Deniall, 70, 90, 111-12, 121, 123,
142, 144, 153; *Dialogue*, 82, 122,
128-29, 130, 137, 153; *A Dia-
logue-Antheme*, 120-21; *The Discharge*, 78, 116, 127, 131, 152,
153, 180; *Discipline*, 5, 38-40,
135, 150, 166; *Divinitie*, 55, 83-
84, 93, 116, 126; *Dooms-day*, 86-
87, 130, 153; *Dotage*, 142, 174;
Dulnesse, 33, 101, 131, 177-78;
Easter, 73, 115, 124, 127, 130;
Easter-wings, 5, 28, 38, 111, 121,
123, 130, 133, 139, 150, 181; *The
Elixir*, 118-20; *Employment* (I),
111, 115; *Employment* (II), 153;
*Ephes. iv. 30. Grieve not the
Holy Spirit*, 38, 84; *Even-song*,
87, 130, 136, 153, 169-71; *Faith*,
5, 74; *The Familie*, 67-69, 90,
116; *The Foil*, 64-65, 116, 120-
21, 131, 174; *The Forerunners*,
85-86, 93, 116, 128, 131, 175-77;
Frailtie, 153; *Giddinesse*, 92, 153;
The Glance, 116, 133, 154-55;
The Glimpse, 52, 85, 128; *Good
Friday*, 130; *Grace*, 38; *Gratefulnesse*, 52, 178; *Grief*, 85, 122,
131, 144; *Heaven*, 33-36, 38, 55,
115, 127; *The Holdfast*, 5, 116,
152; *Home*, 92, 116, 145, 162;
Hope, 101, 121-22, 131, 166;
Humilitie, 25-27, 38, 131; *A true
Hymne*, 129, 177, 181; *The Invitation*, 76, 86, 114, 165; *Jesu*,
120; *The Jews*, 5, 84-85, 116,
120-21; *Jordan* (I), 28-33, 38, 56,
93, 101, 116, 131, 160, 173, 181;
Jordan (II), 29, 80, 117-18, 128,
130, 131, 160, 173, 181; *Josephs
coat*, 5, 93, 116; *Judgement*, 115,
130, 153; *Justice* (I), 121, 152;
Justice (II), 5, 53; *Lent*, 78, 127,

Herbert, George (*continued*):
130; *Life*, 127, 131; *Longing*, 38,
70, 129-30; *Love* (I), 19-20, 37,
38, 57-58, 115, 150; *Love* (II),
19-20, 37, 38, 57-58, 75, 150, 153;
Love (III), 36-37, 38, 115, 128;
Love-joy, 101, 116, 120-21, 130;
Love unknown, 5, 82-83, 131,
144-45, 163; *Man*, 142-44; *Mans
medley*, 116; *Mattens*, 75, 130,
139; *The Method*, 127, 129, 130,
157; *Miserie*, 38, 118; *Mortification*, 139; *Nature*, 153, 158; *Obedience*, 80-81; *The Odour*, 153;
An Offering, 76-77, 82, 127, 137,
153; *Paradise*, 102, 116, 123, 165,
171-72; *A Parodie*, 93, 116, 127;
Peace, 133, 192; *The Pearl*, 37,
44-47, 57, 78-80, 93, 105-106, 116,
138, 142, 150, 153, 181; *The
Pilgrimage*, 84, 129, 165; *The
Posie*, 120-21, 128, 140; *Praise*
(I), 115, 138, 139, 153; *Praise*
(II), 5, 137-38, 175; *Praise* (III),
70, 114, 123, 140, 142; *Prayer*
(I), 42-45, 101, 115; *Prayer* (II),
153; *The Priesthood*, 102; *Providence*, 120, 157, 192; *The Pulley*, 16-19, 38, 98-99, 116, 130,
133, 165, 182; *The Quidditie*,
76, 92, 117; *The Quip*, 92, 116,
131, 139-40; *Redemption*, xv, 5,
98, 117, 128, 154, 159, 165; *Repentance*, 73-74, 159-60; *The
Reprisall*, 96-97, 117, 152, 153;
The Rose, 25, 38, 86, 131; *The
Sacrifice*, 15-16, 55, 66-67, 70, 72-
73, 120, 128, 130, 138, 142, 159;
The H. Scriptures (I), 75, 160-
63; *The H. Scriptures* (II), 75-
76, 165; *The Search*, 70; *Self-
condemnation*, 51-52, 126; *Sepulchre*, 5, 85, 102, 137, 154;
Sighs and Grones, 5, 77-78, 116,
137; *Sinne* (II), 107-108, 115;
The Sinner, 101, 153, 158-59;
Sinnes round, 49-51, 122, 140,
142; *Sion*, 5, 78, 81-82, 178; *The
Size*, 94-95, 116, 127, 152; *The
Sonne*, 59-60, 91, 116, 131, 164;